Depr

MW01129964

Frugality

Tips, Tricks & Life Hacks from the Great Depression Era that We Can Use Today

How to Enjoy Life and Be Comfortable No Matter Your Income, Even in Poverty

By

Deborah Harold

Parma Books

Cover & Book Design by Robin Wright

First Edition

Contents

Introduction to the Great Depression

We are living in a time with uncertainty and a questionable future around every corner. In a way, we are repeating history. So we need to learn from those who lived through and survived previous generations. Our parents, grandparents, and in some cases, great-grandparents survived a period known as the Great Depression.

They did it by living frugally and learning to do things on their own. I've put together some of the lessons learned from my family so you can have a guide to help you survive during these challenging times. But first, let's take a quick look at what the Great Depression was and what people did to live during those times.

The Great Depression was a ten year period in American History from 1929 to 1939. It continues to remain one of the worst economic downturns in American history. In the preceding decade, there was a period of affluence for middle and working-class individuals. This previous boom provided people with more leisure time and started a consumer society. However, the economic depression of the Great

Depression has a major impact on the daily life of families. Much the same as we see happening today on a smaller scale.

At the height of the Great Depression, nearly a quarter of the US workforce was unemployed. Even those who were still employed had a reduction in hours and/or a cut in their wages. Even professionals such as doctors and lawyers saw drops of up to 40% in their income.

The majority of the population was facing financial instability if not complete ruin. As a result, many started living by the motto: "Use it up, wear it out, make do or do without." Many families discovered new ways to live a frugal life. They started gardens, patched clothes, and found cheaper forms of entertainment.

Depression-era homemakers learned to stretch food budgets through smart shopping, meal preparation, and using food scraps wisely. Pot lucks became a way to share food and enjoy the social engagement. People started to spend more time at home and focused on entertainment in the forms of board games and radio.

Many of these hacks and solutions can still be used and applied today. After talking with my family and looking into what other families did during the Great Depression, I've come up with some of the best hacks, tips, and tricks to help you save money, time, and effort in all areas of your life. Let's take a look at these and see what ones you can apply in your life to get through these new difficult times.

Depression-era Life Hacks for Food

The first thing we are going to look at is how you can apply a series of life hacks to help you get the most out of items in your home and how to save time and money doing everyday chores. Let's start by looking at some food hacks that will help you stretch your food budget.

Save Money on Pantry Goods

The first area where you can use depression-era hacks is to stretch your food budget. You can do this by saving money when you shop and making your food go further, you can grow a garden, you can meal plan, and you can stock up a depression-era pantry. Let's look in-depth at each of these areas so you'll be able to get the most out of your food.

When it comes to stretching a food budget, most people think they have to cut out or reduce healthy foods. This isn't the case; there are quite a few healthy foods you can purchase for less than a dollar a serving that can be stretched to make a range of meals and provide you with food for a week or more. Let's look at some of the top healthy foods you can purchase for cheap.

Black Beans

Black beans are high in fiber, calcium, and folic acid. By purchasing them dry and boiling, you will preserve a lot of antioxidants. Cooking them is easy, and you can use them to make soup. You'll often be able to buy the dry beans for less than 30 cents a pound.

Eggs

These are one of the most versatile healthy foods for less than a dollar. There are a variety of ways you can use them. They are a simple breakfast that gives you protein to get your day started. You can also use them to make vegetable frittatas that can be stored for a few days in the refrigerator. Eggs are also an item you can get on your own if you raise chickens.

Almonds

This is a great healthy snack for those on the go. You can often get almonds for about 60 cents a serving of 20 to 25 almonds.

Garbanzo Beans

High in fiber, these are a great addition to salads or can be used to make your own hummus for cheaper than the store-bought option. You can often get about a half cup for about 30 cents or in a can for about a dollar.

Oats

These are very affordable, often about one dollar a pound. Homemade oatmeal is a great cheap breakfast option and can even be used in place of flour to make cookies.

Pinto Beans

Refried beans are cheap and easy to make on your own; and provide more health benefits when you do so. At about 25 cents a half-cup, they add fiber and protein to your diet.

Rice

This has long been a frugal pantry staple. This is especially true if you cook it from scratch. You'll have a range of options to choose from, and most are under a dollar a pound. Rice can be used as a base for dinner, in soups, or as its own side dish. You can cook it in bulk and then use it in meals throughout the week.

Lentils

This is another option, similar to beans. You can get them for less than a dollar a pound. However, these don't require soaking like beans, so they can be prepared in less time. They can be used in soup or make an excellent side dish.

Chicken

Depending on the part of the chicken, this can be a little more expensive than other healthy foods. However, if you want to include meat in your diet, this can be the cheapest option. You can keep chicken in the freezer for up to six months, and it can be used in a wide variety of recipes. You can even use chicken bones to make broth for use in other recipes.

Yogurt

If you want to add calcium and protein to your diet, then yogurt is a great choice. A cup of yogurt will cost about 75 cents to a dollar. You can also save money by making your own yogurt.

Whole Grain Pasta

There are a number of dishes you can make with pasta, and whole-grain pasta makes it healthier. Whole grain pasta comes with a higher nutritional value than regular pasta without costing you a whole lot more.

Popcorn

This is another great healthy snacking option. Plain popcorn can be around a dollar a pound. To keep it healthy, make sure you don't serve it with a lot of salt and butter.

Grapes

This is another fun and affordable snack, especially if you have kids. You can even freeze grapes for a great summertime snack. They are also high in antioxidants.

Bananas

At about 50 cents a pound, you can do a lot with bananas. You can eat them as a snack, add them to breakfast cereal, make banana bread, use them to bulk up smoothies, and more.

Kiwi

As long as you buy kiwi when they are in season or on sale, then you can get them for about 35 cents apiece. These fruits are high in fiber and Vitamin C. They can be eaten plain or added to smoothies and fruit salads.

Watermelon

This is an excellent summertime fruit that is rich in antioxidants. You can eat it plain or use it to make things like juice and popsicles. When you purchase them on sale, you can save a lot of money.

Oranges

At about a dollar a pound, oranges can be a cheaper alternative than orange juice each morning. They also give you a high amount of antioxidants and Vitamin C.

Sweet Potatoes

At about a dollar a pound, these have lots of Vitamin A and are a great alternative to the potato. You can use them to make fries, sweet potato pie, and more. You can truly create a wide range of dishes with these.

Kale

Kale chips are a great alternative to traditional chips and are about 50 cents a cup. Kale can also be added to smoothies for extra Vitamin A, C, and K in your diet.

Broccoli

Nearly any pasta dish can have broccoli added, or it can be eaten as a side dish. Broccoli can even be used as a main course and is about 50 cents a serving.

Beets

At about 90 cents a pound, these are one of the more affordable options. They can be roasted, added to smoothies, or used as a main dish in salads.

Spinach

This is a great addition to salads and smoothies. At about 50 cents per cup, you can use these in a variety of dishes for a healthy addition.

Carrots

These can be a healthy snack option or can be added as a staple to soups and salads. There are also several recipes to use carrots for side dishes.

Milk

Milk has often been raised in cost at times, but when it comes to per-ounce cost, it is still cheaper than juice. A cup of milk will cost less than 20 cents. Avoid buying the more expensive juice and eat fresh fruit instead while drinking milk with your breakfast.

Water

Tap water is one of the cheapest drinks available. Try to avoid flavored drinks and switch to water. It'll be cheaper on your food budget and healthier. Depending on where you live, it may be a good idea to invest in a filter to have safer drinking water.

These are just a few of the general tips to help stretch your food budget. There are some specific things you can do to save on the main staples, such as meat, dairy, seafood, coffee, and produce. Let's look at how you can save money on each of these.

Save Money on Meat

Often one of the largest expenses when it comes to food is meat. There are rarely coupons for meat, and the prices are often variable. There are several things you can do to save money on your next meat purchase.

The main thing is to remember that you can go without meat every once in a while. This may not seem like a way to save on meat, but it is a practical solution if you need to make a cut in your overall food budget. There are plenty of other dishes you can eat for cheap while you save up for your next grocery run when there might be cheaper meat options.

When you look in the meat section, check for peel-off stickers on the meats. These are often great money-saving coupons that can help you get instant money off your meat purchase. You often won't find coupons in the circular ads unless it is around the holiday time. Similarly, you should check the quick sale and manager's special area of the meat department. This is often because they are close to expiring, and you can easily save a lot of money. Either make a meal that day or just freeze until you can plan your next meals.

It can also be a good idea to try alternative cuts of meat you wouldn't normally get. For example, ground turkey may be cheaper than ground beef. Often when used in a recipe, you won't even notice the difference. Another option can be to make your own ground beef. If you see ground chuck on sale, you can buy it in bulk and then grind it with a mixer attachment or ask the meat counter to do it for you. You'll save a lot of money this way.

It also pays to buy in bulk if you can. This often means frozen meats, especially when it comes to chicken. Avoid purchasing frozen meats that contain sodium fillers. If you are going to purchase fresh meats, go for the bigger packages and then divide and freeze yourself. For example, you can buy a whole chicken to make several meals out of and then use the bones for making broth or soups.

Save Money on Dairy

Aside from meat, one of the other main expenses in a grocery budget is dairy items. Oftentimes the cheaper options are full of chemicals and oils that aren't healthy for you. In addition, the prices of dairy products tend to rise when there is difficulty in the economy. So the next time you need to buy dairy items, consider the following to save some money.

Perhaps the easiest way to save on dairy products is by searching for coupons. You'll often find coupons for things like sour cream, yogurt, butter, and cottage cheese. If you do find a coupon or sale deal, then be sure to stock up as much as possible. Milk and butter are easy to freeze and thaw to the same consistency, allowing them to last for a couple months. If you do a lot of baking or home cooking, it is especially important to stock up on butter when its on sale.

Speaking of cooking and baking, save money by using powdered milk in these recipes. Powdered milk is cheaper and is very shelf-stable. While it may taste a bit weird when drinking it straight, you won't notice the difference when using it in cooking or baking.

When it comes to dairy products, you do best to avoid store brands. While this may seem odd, brand name products often have a better sale or coupon deal. Similarly, if you have the option to buy eggs, cheese, and other dairy products from the source, you should do so. You may even be able to raise your own chicken for your own egg source.

Another counterintuitive hack is to buy organic milk. While these may be higher in cost, they are a better choice for those who don't use milk that often. Most organic kinds of milk are ultra-pasteurized and hormone-free, so they last longer. This way, you won't waste money dumping milk that goes bad. Similarly, you want to watch how much milk you are using and look for alternatives if you are going through it too fast.

Lastly, make sure you avoid what is known as convenience foods. Rather than buying yogurt in single-serving tubs, purchase a bulk tub and divide it up on your own. Purchase block cheese and shred it yourself rather than getting the pre-shredded variety. It is more work, but cheaper than paying for the extra packaging.

Save Money on Seafood

Seafood is another option that is very healthy for you, but it can often be quite expensive. When it comes to eating on a budget, most feel they can't afford seafood. No matter what your food budget, there are ways that you can get your seafood for cheap and enjoy a special meal every once in a while.

First, you need to consider going for the seafood varieties

that are cheaper. This is often white, flaky fish varieties such as pollock. Oftentimes, cheaper seafood will taste the same as more expensive seafood with the right seasonings. If you like halibut, try pollock. If you like tuna, try mackerel. These are just a few options for finding a cheaper option.

Another option is to consider frozen over fresh fish. Most seafood comes in frozen form, and they are often quite cheaper than fresh fish, often about 40% less. If you prefer fresh seafood, then consider buying from local warehouse stores. Here you'll find fish in bulk for a fraction of the cost, and you can freeze what you don't eat right away.

Another way to save money is to buy canned seafood. Canned can be a great option if you are going to add the seafood to recipes such as dips, spreads, and salads. It'll be just as tasty and a fraction of the cost.

If you are going to splurge on more expensive seafood, then you should purchase when they are on sale or during the month of March. March tends to be a time when fish is at its lowest price, and if you happen to find expensive fish on sale, you can stock up and freeze for later when prices go back up higher.

Save Money on Coffee

Everyone enjoys a morning cup of coffee. And we've all seen and heard that you can save money by making your own coffee from home. But there are even more ways to save money on this morning staple.

Perhaps the most important thing you can do is to comparison shop. Consider whether it is cheaper at a grocery store versus a warehouse store. Also, keep track of everyday prices so you can determine when it is a good price to stock up on coffee. Similarly, when you shop for coffee, avoid products that are at eye level. Often the most expensive coffees are stocked at eye level, and you can save a couple dollars going for coffee that is higher or lower on the shelf.

Another option is to buy coffee beans in bulk since this is cheaper than pre-packaged coffee. It also gives you the opportunity to make your own unique blend. Most stores will have a coffee grinder, or you can do it at home on your own. You can save even more by getting a cheaper coffee and adding salt to it to decrease bitterness.

Whether you purchase beans or pre-packaged, always look for coupons and sales then stock up when you find a great deal. You can freeze your coffee to help it last longer. If you do freeze coffee, don't thaw and refreeze as too many temperature changes aren't good for the coffee.

Save Money on Produce

Aside from the meat, most are surprised to learn that produce can actually be quite expensive. Thankfully, there are more options for getting fresh produce for cheap than there are other types of food. Let's consider some ways you can save money on your produce budget.

First, always look for coupons. Weekly store ads always have some form of a discount on produce. Plus, other foods may offer coupons for produce if it is used in a recipe, such as soups. Also, message produce companies, and they will often send you coupons for free produce. Following them on social media will also allow you access to manufacturer coupons as well.

Another great idea is to head to the local farmer's markets. Here you'll find fresh, local, and organic produce often at better prices than you'll pay in the grocery store. This is also a reminder that you should always shop for produce that is in season. Produce that is in season will often be cheaper than produce that is out of season. In a moment, I'll provide you with a guide on when to purchase what produce.

Another great way to save money and get fresh produce is to plant a garden. If you grow more produce than you can eat, you have the option to can or freeze the excess for use during the offseason. If you don't have room in your yard for a garden, then look to see if there is a community garden program in your area. If neither of these options is available, you can also contact commercial orchards or farms in your area and see if they offer "pick your own" days where you can get discounts for picking your own produce.

No matter how you get your produce, make sure you stock up whenever you get a good deal. Produce are the perfect items to stock up on since you can freeze, dehydrate, or can the majority of them or turn them into things like sauces, jams, and butter for use throughout the year.

Now that we know how to save money when buying your produce at a store. Let's look a little more closely on how you can save money on produce by growing a garden.

Grow a Garden

Gardening is one of the best ways to save money while putting fresh produce on the table. It was a very popular option during the Great Depression and often involved the whole community working together. In addition, starting a garden is something you can do with very little investment. Consider how much you could save by looking at three examples:

1. Zucchini plants produce 10 pounds per plant but cost about $2 a pound at the store. Saving you $20 a plant.

2. Tomatoes produce 25 pounds per plant but cost about $6 a pound at the store. Saving you $150 a plant.

3. Bell peppers produce 4 pounds per plant but cost about $7.50 a pound at the store. Saving you $30 a plant.

With just these three plants alone, you can save almost $200 by planting your own garden. If you are going to start your own garden, there are ten top vegetables that give you the best return and are easy to maintain:

1. Tomatoes

2. Broccoli

3. Peas

4. Green Beans

5. Carrots

6. Spinach

7. Lettuce

8. Cucumbers

9. Pumpkins

10. Kale

With these benefits, you can see why starting a garden is a great idea. So now, let's look at how you can get started with your garden.

Cultivating a Full Outdoor Garden

Starting a garden doesn't have to be a costly or involved

endeavor. There are plenty of depression-era tips that will help you to frugally start a garden and gain the wonderful benefits of having one in your backyard.

The first thing you need to do when starting a garden is to carefully plan out what you want to grow and the season in which you will be growing it. You should only grow produce that makes the most sense for your needs and the area where you are living. Often people don't have a lot of space, so you'll need to use what you have carefully. Also, make sure you only grow enough to cover what you'll eat. If you grow something no one will eat, then you are only wasting food and space.

Similarly to planning your garden space, you also want to plan out what you will do when the harvest is ready. When the harvest is coming, plan out dinners that feature your harvested produce like soups and casseroles. You will be limited in what you can do, but this is a money-saving habit that helped many depression-era gardeners. If you can't use all of what your garden produces, then you should have a plan in place for canning or freezing excess produce for use later in the year.

For this reason, you want to plant some fall harvest

vegetables that will last well in storage. There are plenty of vegetables that you can harvest in the fall, like potatoes, turnips, and carrots. Root vegetables like these will extend your gardening season and will stay fresh as long as you can store them around 50 degrees.

You can also extend your gardening time by building a cold frame. This will allow you to garden most crops well into and potentially through winter. You can build one yourself from repurposed items to save even more money.

Save money on the soil for your garden by making your own compost. This is a great way to have an organic garden on a budget. Create your own compost bin and add things then mix into your soil when tilling your garden at the start of the planting season. As the season progresses, add more around your plants and hand mix with a hoe or rake in order to add nutrients to the soil to help your plants grow. Some excellent items of include in your compost bin include the following:

- Peels from fruits and vegetables

- Coffee grounds

- Crushed eggshells

- Clippings from leaves and grass

- Shredded newspaper

- Plant clippings like dead leaves, buds, etc.

When you are ready to plant, there are a few sources for your seeds. If you do have more room to plant extra plants, then you may want to consider ordering your seeds online in bulk. This often lowers the price if you can buy in larger quantities. Even if you don't have a large garden area see if others in your area are into gardening, and you can go in on a seed purchase together.

Another option is to get your seeds through an exchange or library. Many public libraries have a seed exchange, but you can also find local individuals to swap with. Look in local community listings to see if there is an option near you. In addition, local seeds will be better and easier to grow since they are adapted to your local area.

Lastly, you can choose to start your own seedling indoors from previously grown produce. There are a number of seed starter kits you can use, but the concept is simple. You want to start growing seeds in a bit of soil indoors until they are a stronger plant and then transplant them outside in your garden. You should ideally start your seedlings about a month to a month and a half before you expect the last frost. When growing seedlings indoors, there are a few tips to follow:

- Ensure the seeds have enough moisture and drainage.

- Keep the seedlings near a window, so they get a lot of light. Most plants need at least 12 hours of light.

- At night, cover the plants to keep them moist and encourage strong growth.

As you transplant your seedlings outside, you need to take good care of them as they grow. Make sure you regularly prune and weed the garden. Plants should be staked and trained to climb as needed. Nurture your plants regularly in order to yield hearty crops that make your garden financially worthwhile.

You can also use free gardening supplies to save money. Repurpose items you would normally throw away rather than spending money on gardening tools. For example, a milk jug can be cut down to create a scoop for the soil, and you can use the box-spring from an old bed to make a trellis for vines to grow. The more items you can get for free, the less you have to spend.

Lastly, as you harvest your crops, make sure you save seeds for the next year. This will save you money on seeds the following spring. Some vegetables aren't that easy, but many plants are ideal for this. The following thirteen vegetables practically regrow themselves:

1. Scallions

2. Garlic

3. Romaine Lettuce

4. Carrots

5. Basil

6. Lemongrass

7. Celery

8. Onions

9. Bok Choy

10. Avocado

11. Sweet Potatoes

12. Ginger

13. Pineapple

If you don't have space to plant a garden, you can still take advantage of the money savings by growing your own food. You'll just need to do it with a container garden.

Container Gardening

Container gardening is a great way to grow even just a few vegetables to make produce a little more affordable at the store. It is largely the same as regular gardening, just on a smaller scale. There are a few tips that can help you have success with your container garden.

- Keep your containers light and easy to move while also saving money on the soil by fill the pot half full of chopped up pool noodles, crushed boxes, Styrofoam, or something similar. This will also assist with drainage.

- Ensure the containers you use have proper drainage. Holes in the pots, along with a layer of rock or other material, will help enable drainage.

- Don't use garden soil, but rather use potting soil for best results in a container garden.

- Make sure you repot your plants as they outgrow a planter and, if possible, switch out the soil each year.

- Once a month, you should fertilize your containers.

- Put an uncooked unbroken egg at the bottom of your container; it will provide fertilizer as it decomposes.

- Since a potted plant will dry faster, you should use a plastic liner and a soil mix that retains water in order to keep the soil moist. Clean diapers in the bottom of a pot is another good option.

- When choosing containers for your garden, you can repurpose any number of containers into plant pots.

Nearly all vegetables can be grown in containers. Some of the best plants for this form of gardening include the following:

- Tomatoes

- Chili Peppers

- Salad Greens

- Radishes

- Carrots

- Potatoes

- Onions

- Herbs

One last thing that I need to mention is succession planting. This is a great way to get more food from your garden and ensure you have a steady food supply.

Succession Planting

Gardening is a relatively easy way to get food. However, if you are using it as a source of food, you may not want to wait until harvest time for your entire crop. Wouldn't it be great to have food continuously available throughout the summer? The best way to grow more food is through succession planting. This is a process where you grow the same plant continually in the same space throughout the growing season.

The best example of succession planting is lettuce. Start by planting your lettuce seeds over a seedling mix and water well. You can start harvesting baby leaves in about two to three weeks. Every week you can add more seeds to the same seedling mix. This means you will be able to harvest lettuce each week as you plant more seeds. When it comes to lettuce, this only works for those that don't need to grow a head.

Succession planting is also great for carrots and radishes. With these, you sow seeds every two to three weeks rather than seeding weekly. Simply plant another seed in the hole after harvesting a carrot or radish. When you succession plant in either of these ways, you'll double the harvest from your crops.

Another option of succession planting is to stagger your planting schedule. For example, if you plant tomatoes the first day, then they will all ripen at the same time. You can start your tomato seeds a couple weeks apart so that plants will ripen at alternating times.

These plants can be succession planted.

7 Day Interval Plants

- Lettuce

  - Mesclun

  - Loose-leaf

  - Romaine

  - Radicchio

- Spinach

14 Day Interval Plants

- Beets

- Kale

- Kohlrabi

- Tomatoes

- Carrots

- Radish

- Peas

- Bush Beans

- Turnips

- Potatoes

21 Day Interval Plants

- Arugula

- Carrots

- Cucumbers

- Melons

- Squash

No matter how you grow your produce, another aspect of

depression-era savings is to use your produce effectively and have it available year-round. Let's look at two ways you can get the most out of your produce.

Making the Most Out of Your Produce

Once you harvest your fruits and vegetables, you'll want to make the excess last as long as possible. There are two ways to do this: freezing and canning. Let's look a little more closely at how you can do these two methods.

Freezing Fruits and Vegetables

If you find yourself with an abundance of produce at the end of the harvest season, then you need to preserve it as fresh as possible until you can use it. One great way to do this is through freezing. Let's look at how this is done.

First, you need to prepare your produce for freezing. To do this, wash the produce thoroughly, removing all leaves, stems, and pits. Chop your vegetables into a desired shape/size. For example, potatoes do best when sliced, shredded, and cubed. Carrots are best in coins. Peppers and onions do best in strips. It is also important to note that the best vegetables for freezing are carrots, potatoes, peppers, green peas, corn, zucchini, squash, and onions.

When it comes to firmer vegetables such as green beans, asparagus, broccoli, cauliflower, potatoes, and snap peas, you'll need the added step of blanching. You can do this by submerging them in boiling water for three minutes. When you remove them from the boiling water, immediately plunge them into ice water for the same period of time. Blot the produce dry before freezing.

Freezing fruits is slightly different. The best fruits for freezing are strawberries, bananas, peaches, cherries, and blueberries. When preparing fruits, you should peel or slice/chop the larger fruits, such as apples and peaches. You can often freeze fruits without boiling first. It is best to freeze your fruit in measured amounts using gallon bags. This way, you only remove enough for a pie or a shake. It is important to keep in mind that fruit will lose its firm texture when frozen, so it is best to use frozen fruit for pureed or baked recipes once thawed.

The best herbs for freezing are cilantro, dill, mint, parsley, basil, and chives. Herbs will need to be blanched in boiling water for five to ten seconds. Dip in ice water at the same time and pat dry. You can dice herbs before freezing. A great option is to freeze herbs in an ice-cube tray with some water or homemade stock for bullion. Herbs are good for four to six months when frozen.

If you don't want to freeze your produce or don't have room to keep a lot of items in the freezer, then consider the second option of canning your produce.

Canning

Canning was a large part of depression-era life. Leftover produce can be canned as jams, salsas, sauces, purees, and fermented foods. Canning is a very delicate endeavor since improper canning can lead to botulism. However, if you follow proper canning guidelines, you'll be safe and have plenty of food throughout the year. Visit the National Center for Home Food Preservation for the latest guidelines and to get detailed instructions on how to properly can food.

In addition to preserving food, you can also save money with depression-era cooking tips. This can include proper use of food scraps, planning ahead with meal planning, and cooking from depression-era recipes. Let's first look at some cooking tips learned from previous generations.

Cooking Tips

When it comes to depression-era food saving, there was a lot of preserving and substituting; but there were also tips on cooking that helped make food stretch. They knew how to use food scraps properly, they planned out meals in advance to use all the ingredients available, and they made very simple recipes. Let's look at some tips in all of these areas to see how they can be applied today.

Using Food Scraps

Households in the United States waste more food than anywhere else along the food supply chain. This waste is estimated at 27 million tons. That is a lot of food to be wasted, and it happens for five main reasons:

1. People often purchase food with the intention of cooking and eating, but through a lack of planning, the food spoils or expires before it can be eaten. Also, if people choose to eat out rather than a planned meal at home can cause food to go bad.

2. Food also goes bad when it is stored improperly, whether it is in a place that is too cold, hot, moist, or dry.

3. Buying more food than you can cook and eat before it spoils is another main reason.

4. Food can be discarded prematurely because people are confused by label dates on food and what they really mean.

5. Lastly, not using leftovers to their fullest potential can be a cause of discarding spoiled foods.

One of the best ways to reduce and eliminate food waste is to change your habits and routines. This means buying less, using more of what you have on hand, and saving a bit of extra money in the process. Your circumstances will determine exactly what you can do, but the following are some tips to help you use your food scraps wisely.

Buy What You Can Use

After preparing a week's worth of meals, you'll likely have a little bit of everything leftover in the refrigerator. Rather than throwing these foods out, use them up. Consider some ideas:

- Save produce for use in soups later.

- Extra cucumber can be used as a refreshing flavor for water.

- Use milk nearing expiration to make tea or other foods that can be preserved.

- Leftover lemons can be used for cleaning purposes.

- Onions, garlic, and other such leftovers can be used to add savor to food dishes.

- Apples can be made into applesauce or dessert-like apple pie.

Leftovers can also be repurposed in a variety of ways. Cooked vegetables can be used in a variety of ways for other meals, as side dishes or stock for soups. Some examples of produce scraps you can reuse instead of throwing away include the following:

- Peels, ends, and cores.

- Tough outer leaves from cauliflower and cabbage.

- Root vegetable tops such as carrots and beets.

- Mushroom stems.

- Brown or mushy pieces of fruit.

- Small amounts of leftovers that can be made into another meal.

While these may seem like nothing more than garbage waste to some, they can be used, and some nourishment gained if you know what to do.

Soup Containers

After each meal, add your odds and ends to a container stored in the freezer. Eventually, there will be enough in the container to make a soup. Make sure you have enough room in your freezer for a larger container and then put all meat, vegetable, and gravy leftovers into it. Once the container is full, you can put all the contents into a pot with some stock and cook it into a soup. This can be tastier than you may think as long as you follow a few simple tips:

- Avoid conflicting flavors and spices. To do this, you should stick to just basic ingredients like plain meat, potatoes, and vegetables.

- Use a good stock for cooking your soup. Leftovers often don't provide enough flavor, so you'll need a good stock as your soup base.

- Adjust your ingredients as needed. If you don't have enough ingredients in your container, you can always add more. If you have extra vegetables from a harvest or you have canned beans, rice, or paste, these can all help add to the soup. Another option is to add salt, pepper, and other spices.

- Protect your food scraps; they will keep in the freezer for a long time but won't keep forever. When you start a new batch of scraps, add a new label with the date. If three months have passed and the container isn't full, then you should make the soup anyway.

Another alternative is to use the contents of the soup container to make a pot pie. Spoon everything into a pie crust with vegetables first, meat second, and then enough broth to cover them. If you don't have broth, you can use bouillon to make some. Cover the dish with a second crust and bake at 350 degrees Fahrenheit until brown.

Some of the best items to keep in a soup container or stock bag, including the following:

- Carrot peels

- Potato peels

- Celery leaves

- Peapods

- Mushroom stems

- Onion ends

- Corn cobs

There are some vegetables that shouldn't be used for soups and stocks because of their strong flavor. This would include the following:

- Cabbage

- Turnips

- Rutabagas

- Broccoli

- Artichokes

Side Dishes

Often the pieces of vegetables that people feel need to be wasted can be the healthiest and tastiest portion of the food, such as the green tops of carrots and beets, or the stalks of leafy vegetables. Some of the options you can use include the following:

- Carrot Tops - A pungent and herbal flavor.

- Radish Tops - Peppery, but milder than the radish itself.

- Turnip Greens - A slightly bitter flavor.

- Beet Greens - A mild sweet taste.

- Onion Tops - A slightly stronger flavor than scallions.

- Fennel Stalks and Fronds - A delicate, licorice-like flavor.

- Stalks of Greens - Often the same flavor as the leaves.

Young and tender scraps can be used in salads while larger and tougher scraps can be added to stir-fries or sautéed to make a side dish. You can also use them to make a soup or quiche.

Smoothies

When it comes to fruit scraps, smoothies make great options to avoid waste. They are very easy to make; simply use whatever you have and blend it with any type of milk, yogurt, or another creamy treat. With smoothies, you also don't have to worry about the condition of the fruit since the texture won't matter once you blend it. If the fruit isn't sweet enough, you can add a little sweetener.

Lunches

The simplest way to avoid food waste is to turn leftovers into lunch for the next day. Simply reheat the next day, or if you don't want the same thing two days in a row, you can save it for the next day. You can even use a reusable container to take the leftovers to work for a brown bag lunch.

If you prefer a fresh dish, you can combine your leftovers with fresh ingredients to have something new. Add chicken to a salad or cheese to potatoes. If you have a larger amount of leftovers, you can freeze some for a second dinner later.

Frozen Meals

If you don't think you can eat leftovers within a few days, then you can put them in a freezer-safe container and store them. Some good containers for freezing leftovers include:

- Pyrex Bowls

- Mason Jars

- Plastic Containers

- Ziploc Bags

- Freezer Wrap

Always make sure you label containers with the contents and the freezing date, so you'll be able to eat them while they're still good. Some leftovers are only good for one to six months. The following is a list of foods that freeze well:

- Avocados - Puree and freeze them for a healthy addition to leftovers.

- Baked Goods - Make a double batch and freeze the rest for breakfast or snacks.

- Baking Supplies - Flour and sugar can be kept safe in the freezer.

- Beans - Buy in bulk, cook, and then freeze for use in recipes later to avoid the cost of canned beans.

- Block Cheese - Cheese can be frozen up to six months, but if you want to prevent it from crumbling, you should shred it before freezing.

- Broccoli - Soak in saltwater for about ten minutes to kill any insects. Blanch for four minutes and then freeze.

- Celery - You'll lose the crunch but not the flavor. Use frozen celery to add to casseroles and soups.

- Corn on the Cob - Leave the husk on and place it in an airtight bag. Simply add boiling water or microwave for five minutes.

- Eggs - Put eggs into ice-cube trays and freeze in a bag. You can thaw them in the refrigerator when you are ready to use them.

- Fruit - Nearly all fruits can be frozen, but they will get a little soggy. Frozen fruit is best used in smoothies or baking.

- Herbs - Nearly all herbs freeze well. Place them in an ice-cube tray with water or stock and then add them to a casserole, soup, or another recipe.

- Milk - Make sure you pour out a little first to account for expansion. Milk can be frozen for up to six months. The same can be done with butter, cream cheese, and yogurt.

- Meat/Poultry - This is a great freezer item. Repackage the meat in freezer bags, and they will last up to 12 months.

- Mushrooms - Sauté and then freeze mushrooms. You can then add them directly to recipes.

- Onions - Frozen onions can be added directly to recipes from their frozen state.

- Nuts - Freezing nuts is easy and prevents them from going rancid.

- Peppers - Dice them or cut them into strips for addition to future recipes.

- Rice - In an air-tight container, rice can be frozen for up to a year. It also prevents pest infestation. Rice can also be frozen after cooking.

- Spinach - Rinse and blanch for two minutes before freezing. In freezer bags, it will last up to nine months.

- Tomatoes - These do very well in the freezer. You can also roast them first before freezing.

No matter what you are freezing, use the following tips for freezing food:

- You can pre-assemble ingredients before freezing for easy addition to crock-pots.

- Packaging your food determines how well it will do in the freezer. Remove as much air as possible. If you have a vacuum sealer, this is best.

- Warm food should be cooled down to room temperature before freezing.

- Stock up on freezer paper, heavy-duty Ziploc bags, foil, and plastic wrap in order to properly freeze food.

- Repackage any meat before freezing if you aren't going to use it within one to two months.

- Clearly mark all frozen items, so you'll know what you froze and how long it is good for.

- Always thaw frozen foods in the refrigerator or microwave.

Understanding What Expiration Dates Mean

The USDA estimates that about 20% of food waste comes

from confusion over the expiration date printed on items. A product's sell-by or expiration date is a recommendation for quality, not safety. Except in the case of infant formula, food dating is voluntary and not a federal requirement. This has led to a lot of confusion. Understand what the labels mean to avoid wasting food:

- Best if Used By/Before - This is a time frame to indicate the best flavor or quality of the labeled product.

- Sell By - This is how long a store has to display the product for inventory management.

- Use By - This is the last recommended date for using the product at peak quality.

- Freeze By - This the last date you can freeze a product in order to maintain peak quality.

With this understanding, if you handle and store food correctly, it can often be used well after the date has passed. Use your own best judgment when determining if food is safe to eat. Don't risk illness and discard any food that smells bad or doesn't look right. However, there are some foods that you can revive and consume.

Stale baked goods and crispy items like bread, cereal, chips, and popcorn can be revived in an oven or microwave rather than being discarded.

- Cereal - Spread the cereal on a baking sheet in a single layer and cook at 350 degrees for five to ten minutes. Watch carefully for burning. After a few minutes, take it out to cool. Once cooled, it will be crisp and can be good for another couple of days.

- Popcorn - Preheat the oven to 250 degrees Fahrenheit and spread the popcorn in a single layer on a baking sheet. Toast it for five minutes.

- Crackers and Tortilla Chips - Preheat the oven to 225 degrees Fahrenheit. Spread a single layer on a cookie sheet and toast for 15 to 25 minutes, flip halfway through. The time will vary depending on the thickness of the food and the crisping you desire. Watch closely to make sure it doesn't burn.

- Bread - Stale bread can be used to make croutons for salads or soups. Cut the bread into cubes and place them in a large bowl. Drizzle with olive oil, salt, and pepper or any other seasoning you prefer. Preheat the oven to 375 degrees Fahrenheit and line a baking sheet with parchment paper. Spread the cubes in an even layer and bake for fifteen to twenty minutes, tossing halfway through and cooking until golden brown.

Another way to avoid food waste while saving money is through proper meal planning. In the depression-era, this was almost an art form, and it is becoming popular again. I'll show you how to do it right so you can get the most out of your food.

Meal Planning

Many view meal planning as a time consuming and costly endeavor that isn't worth the effort. However, it is not something new, and many families used it during the Great Depression to extend the cost savings of their food. It may be a little overwhelming at first, but I'm going to give you five easy steps that will make the process much easier for you.

Find Recipes

The first thing you need to do is come up with a large selection of recipes. Look through cookbooks and online recipes to find your selection. Be sure to choose ones that you and your family will enjoy, but also don't be afraid to move out of your comfort zone in order to try new things. After you have your recipes, find a way to keep them organized. There isn't one specific way; it just needs to work for you.

Plan Your Menu

Once you have your recipes, you can start planning a menu. Menus can span one week to a month or longer. The best money-saving option is to create a plan for a month. Start with a sheet of paper labeled for breakfast, lunch, dinner, and snacks. Then under each have numbers one to thirty. Write down a different recipe under each number. For example, you may have cereal listed for each day of the week except weekends. Lunch may include sandwiches, salad, and soup recipes. The bulk of meal planning is focused on your dinner recipes. Once you have a complete list, you are ready for the next phase.

Develop a Grocery List

Based on the recipes on your list, start putting together a grocery list. Write down what you need and how much you need to cook all of the recipes on your list. Having a complete list means you won't have to run out to the store for each dinner. Once you have a complete list, you can head out shopping. When you come home, put your groceries away. Don't worry about fixing things or putting things together on the same day as shopping; it's a little too much to do in one day.

Prepare Ahead of Time

Gather all your recipes and decide what parts you can prepare in advance. Do as much as you can. For example, if recipes call for ground beef, you can brown all the ground beef needed at one time. The goal is to complete as much of your monthly cooking in a single day as you can.

Follow Your Plan

The last step in the process is to keep your recipes and monthly plan on hand for easy references. After you finish a recipe, cross it off the list. This will help you keep track of what you have cooked. Having an organized system will save you on time. Planning ahead also saves you money on your groceries because you aren't having to go shopping for last-minute items.

In addition to having a meal plan, people in the Great Depression also made use of simple recipes that use as little ingredients as possible. While not an exhaustive list, let's look at just a few examples of depression-era recipes to get you started on the road to proper meal planning.

Depression-era Recipes

Just to give you an example of what a depression-era recipe is, take a look at a few examples. You can find an endless number of depression-era recipes online that will help you get the most out of your food and turn one meal into many while saving you a lot of money on your groceries.

Milk Toast

Ingredients:

- ☐ 4 toast slices

- ☐ 4 butter pats

- ☐ 1 tsp sugar and cinnamon

- ☐ ½ cup milk

Directions:

1. On low, heat the milk.

2. Butter the toast and sprinkle with sugar/cinnamon mix.

3. Tear into bite-sized pieces and place into two bowls.

4. Pour warm milk over the toast pieces.

Depression Bread

Ingredients:

- ☐ 5 lb. all-purpose flour

- ☐ 5 tbsp yeast

- ☐ 6 tsp salt

☐ 6 cups warm water

Directions:

1. Place flour in a large bowl.

2. Make a well in the center.

3. Add yeast to the well and enough water to dissolve the yeast.

4. Once the yeast is dissolved, start adding more water and mixing in the flour until a dough forms.

5. Knead the dough in the bowl a bit.

6. Allow the dough to rise in a warm place with a towel loosely over the top.

7. Once the dough has risen to double in size, punch down the dough and divide it into seven loaves.

8. Shape the loaves and place in loaf pans.

9. Allow the dough to rise for sixty minutes or until doubled in size.

10. Make slits in the top of the dough.

11. Bake at 350 degrees Fahrenheit until brown on top or about 25 minutes based on the oven.

Creamed Chipped Beef on Toast

Ingredients:

- ☐ 2 tbsp butter

- ☐ 2 tbsp all-purpose flour

- ☐ 1 ½ cups warm milk

- ☐ 1 8 oz jar dried beef

- ☐ 1 pinch cayenne pepper or another seasoning

Directions:

1. Over low heat, melt butter in a medium saucepan.

2. Whisk in the flour all at once to form a roux.

3. Whisk in the milk a little bit at a time while increasing the heat to medium-high.

4. Cook while stirring until thickened.

5. Bring to a boil, stir in the beef and seasoning.

6. Heat through and serve over toast.

White Bean and Ham Soup

Ingredients:

- ☐ 1 lb. white navy beans

- ☐ 2 chopped onions

- ☐ 2 cups chopped ham or something similar

- ☐ Water to cover

- ☐ Salt and pepper or another seasoning to taste

Directions:

1. Soak the beans overnight or using the quick soak method.

2. Using a large stockpot, combine beans, onion, and ham.

3. Cover with water by one and a half-inch.

4. Bring to a boil, then reduce the heat to a simmer. Cover partially and simmer for two hours or so. At least until the beans are tender.

5. Watch the water level and add more as needed.

6. Taste and add seasoning as desired.

Sugar Milk Pie

Ingredients:

☐ 3 cups brown sugar

☐ ¼ cup granulated sugar

☐ ⅓ cup flour

☐ 1 ¾ cup milk or cream

☐ 8-inch pie shell

Directions:

1. Mix all ingredients thoroughly together.

2. Pour into the pie shell.

3. Dot with butter and sprinkle on cinnamon and sugar if desired.

4. Bake at 425 degrees Fahrenheit for ten minutes.

5. Reduce temperature to 350 degrees Fahrenheit and bake for forty minutes.

Building a Depression-era Pantry

One key to living frugally and preparing for a depression type event is to prepare and build an adequate pantry. This often is going to look different from your current pantry. Back during the Great Depression, there wasn't a lot of pre-packaged foods or snacks. However, turning your current pantry into one more like our relatives had will save you a lot of money and allow you to make more items on your own. Let's look at some tips to help you build a pantry from the depression-era.

Stock the Basics

There weren't a lot of extras or packaged goods, and most of what made up pantries are things we often purchase in bulk today. This means buying more ingredients rather than ready-made food. The following is a list of some basics to consider keeping on hand:

- Flour for making bread or using as fillers.

- Honey for sweetener.

- Salt for seasoning.

- Cornmeal for making things like grits and cornbread.

Where you live will often determine what is easily available. You can buy most of these and other similar items in bulk at grocery stores. When deciding what to stock in your pantry, avoid pre-made mixes as much as possible.

Stock Up on Beans

Since meat is often expensive and in a depression, you may not be able to afford it as a part of every meal; you'll need to find another source of protein or at least a way to make meat last longer. You can do this by making casseroles, soups, and skillet meals. The best way to save money on these recipes is to use beans. Purchasing dried beans is often cheaper than canned beans. Cooking with dried beans isn't that difficult and offers several options.

Keep Seasonings on Hand

Spices are a good thing to have on hand when cooking your own meals. Since most depression-era recipes were very basic, seasonings can be used to add a variety of flavor. You can also choose to save more money by growing your own herbs and dehydrating them for use later.

Dehydrate Whatever You Can

This is a great way to use extra supplies and not let food go to waste. It is also a way to create shelf-stable foods. Purchase a dehydrator, and it will pay for itself as you dehydrate foods that can then last for months in your pantry.

Now that we've discussed a variety of ways to use depression-era tactics to save money on food let's consider some other areas where our relatives learned to do with less and live frugally. Let's consider clothing and how you can reduce what you have and make it last longer.

Depression-era Life Hacks for Clothing

Clothing is an item that can be costly. Especially if you live in areas with seasons, and you need multiple types of clothing throughout the year. However, if you want to live frugally and save money, you need to do three things to help reduce your clothing budget. First, we'll look at how you can develop a minimalist wardrobe. Then we'll look at how you can make your clothes last longer. Lastly, we'll look at how you can purchase cheap clothes at the thrift store when you really need to replace your clothing items.

Developing a Minimalist Wardrobe

You can save both money and time by adopting a minimalist wardrobe. It isn't boring; rather, it just makes things easier and allows you to be less consumer-focused. You'll be okay with the basics and happy. Let's look at some ways you can simplify your life and adopt a minimalist wardrobe.

First, it is important to define what a minimalist wardrobe is. While we are talking about having less to choose from, you should also ensure that you have pieces that go well together and can be easily mixed and matched. It does mean that you don't need to have a pair of shoes for each outfit or a handbag for each outfit or ten black dresses for each occasion.

For some, this process may be more difficult than for others. This is especially true if you enjoy shopping for clothes. However, it will make it easier for you to get ready to go out in public since you won't have to spend time deciding what to wear.

The first thing you need to do is take a good look at what you currently have. Start by just removing the items you no longer wear. Or you may choose to look through the wardrobe with an eye towards what types of functions they serve.

From there, you can start pairing things down and get rid of the rest. Do you have articles of clothing that don't go with anything else? Are there articles of clothing that don't fit anymore or need repairs? These are some of the easy options to downsize. The idea is to downsize only to items that can easily go with other articles of clothing and/or accessories.

Another option for reducing your clothing is to base it on the colors you prefer to wear. For example, if you prefer to wear black, white, and grey, then every piece in your wardrobe should match these colors.

Having a minimalist wardrobe doesn't mean you need to only have cheap and basic clothing. It is best to focus on quality over quantity. If you can only have a few great articles of clothing, that is better than having extra lower-priced articles of clothing that are lower in quality. Higher quality clothing is also likely to hold up longer and require less frequent replacement.

Once you have your clothing downsized, you can focus on reducing your accessories. Accessories are important to make sure plain clothes have a fashionable flair. For example, have a few scarves to add flair to basic shirts and sweaters. You can also focus on undershirts that are solid or neutral colors to go with a range of clothing.

Lastly, you should set a goal and stick with it. Determine how much clothing you want to keep in your closet and stay there; only purchase new clothes as something becomes worn out and needs to be replaced. When you are tempted to purchase more clothing, you should think of what you have and determine if you really need the extra article of clothing. Make sure you only purchase clothing that is going to pair with at least three articles of clothing already in your closet.

Developing a minimalist clothing system makes this area of your life more convenient, but it also saves you money since you won't be tempted to stay up to date with the latest trends. However, another way to focus on saving money is to extend the life of the clothes you choose to keep.

Make Your Clothes Last Longer

Another great way to save money on clothes is to keep the

clothes you have in great shape. If you want to keep your clothes looking great longer, then you should consider the following seven great depression tips to help your clothes last longer.

Follow Care Instructions

Take the time to read the care instructions and follow them. This not only helps your clothes keep looking nice, but also helps them to last a lot longer. For example, drying an article of clothing on the heat when it says, "tumble dry low" will cause the fibers to break down easier.

Make Your Own Repairs

Mending clothes is something most don't do anymore. However, it is an important skill that most should know in order to get the longest life out of your clothing. This doesn't mean you need the skills to sew entire articles of clothing; you just need to know enough to mend a hole or replace a button. This will help make your clothes last longer.

Wash Inside Out and Close Zippers

Leaving a zipper open can cause ripped clothing due to the

motion of the washer as it agitates. Also, turning clothes inside out when washing will reduce pilling on the visible side so your clothes will continue to look nice.

Wash Black Clothes Separate

Washing your dark clothing together helps prevent fading. Dark clothes have a dye that tends to wash out in the water. When you wash black and dark clothing together, it will prevent the dye from being picked up by other clothes.

Avoid Fabric Softeners

While fabric softeners can make your clothing seem softer and smell better, they can also be damaging to your clothes. Most fabric softeners cause a buildup on clothing, which prevents them from breathing or get completely clean after you wash them.

Use the Right Hangers

Using just regular hangers can damage clothing, especially if you use the cheap plastic kind. Rather spend a little extra getting quality wood or velvet hangers, so your clothes hang naturally. This prevents stretching of the necks, shoulders, and collars, so your clothes hold their shape longer.

Sort Your Laundry

Just as you wash dark clothes together, washing all your clothing according to type is important. When you wash clothes together, you are able to keep them in their proper wash cycles and prevent them from becoming faded or dull.

Despite your best efforts to downsize and maintain a minimalist wardrobe, there is going to come a time when you need to purchase some articles of clothing. If this is the case, you can still be frugal by purchasing certain wardrobe staples at thrift stores.

Thrift Store Wardrobe Purchases

There are a few simple wardrobe staples to have on hand that allow you to create numerous outfits for a fraction of the cost. This can make your outfits easy to plan while also stretching your budget. A great source for these wardrobe staples is your local thrift store, but you will need time and patience in order to find them. Let's look at the four staples you should have on hand to help you keep a minimalist wardrobe and stretch your budget by buying at a local thrift store.

The Black Skirt

No matter what style of black skirt you prefer, having one on hand makes it easy to both dress up and down based on the occasion. You can pair it with a simple t-shirt and sandals to have a casual outfit, or you can pair it with a fancy top and jewelry for an eveningwear look.

A Denim Jacket

You can pair this with a skirt or sundress if you want to wear something into the evening or on a slightly cooler day. The denim jacket is very versatile, so you can pair them with a number of outfit choices.

Grey Dress Pants

These are a functional option for both dressing up and down, depending on the occasion. The dark color of these pants is also a forgiving and slimming appearance. They should also be able to wear and wash well. Dress up for work or dinner by pairing with heels and a dressy top. You can also easily tailor them yourself in order to get a nice fit.

White Dress Shirt

A basic white dress shirt is another versatile option. You can add color through accessories like jewelry. And a white shirt can easily go with any kind of pants, a skirt, or even jeans.

Black Flats

This is something that will never go out of style. You should find a pair that is comfortable and mixes well with both jeans and dress pants. A simple pair will come in handy, so when you find a pair that fits, be sure to buy them.

Infinity Scarves

These can be worn in a variety of ways and can completely change the look of an outfit. Often scarves can be purchased for just a dollar, so at thrift stores, so you should pick them up when you find one. This is the one item of clothing you can have several of since they are small and don't take up a lot of room. Have multiple colors and patterns on hand that can compliment all of your outfits.

Dark Denim Jeans

Nothing is better than a pair of well-fitting jeans. A darker color is best since it wears well and is slimming. You can also tailor your jeans, so they are the perfect length and have a nice fit. It is best to find a quality brand, so you know it is made with quality materials that will last for a while.

When you need to add to your wardrobe, head to your local thrift store and look for these seven staples. It will stretch your budget and allow you to keep your wardrobe in the minimalist style.

In addition to food and clothing, another way to save money is on your home cleaning. There are plenty of cheap cleaning options, and you can even make your own products. Let's consider how you can do this.

Depression-era Life Hacks for Cleaning

When it comes to cleaning your house, you may not think of being frugal. After all, you simply need to buy a cleaning product and then clean your house, right? With depression-era tips, you can learn to clean your home naturally and frugally. You can clean with vinegar, baking soda, and borax. You can also save money by making your own homemade cleaning products.

Cleaning Naturally and Frugally

A lot of people are under the impression you need to use chemicals to clean your home. However, there are plenty of natural products you can use to clean your home. Best of all, most of these products are budget-friendly and allow you to stretch your household cleaning budget. Let's first look at the various natural cleaning products you can use in your home, then we'll look closer at the main three options.

Salt

Salt may not be the first thing you think of when it comes to cleaning, but it does have some uses around the home, including the following:

- Salt is a great natural carpet stain remover. Paired with club soda, it can remove nearly any stain from the carpet. Pour club soda on the stain first and then use the salt to dry out the stain and club soda. The salt can be vacuumed once everything is dry.

- Salt can be used as a general absorber for spills.

- Mixing salt and water together can help shine metal for your tarnished copper items.

- There are also a lot of other frugal uses for salt around your home.

Lemons

Lemons are great for fighting bacteria. Just a few drops of lemon juice can clean sinks, disposals, and counters. Lemon juice can also be added to vinegar to make a cleaning solution or into a powder paste solution to make it even more effective. Consider just a few uses for cleaning with lemons:

- Lemon juice and baking soda can be great to shine metal.

- A cut-up lemon on a stained cutting board makes a great scrubber that removes stains. Wash with warm and soapy water after, and you'll have a cutting board as good as new.

- Plain lemon juice can be used to clean any stainless steel in the house.

- A few teaspoons of lemon juice can be added to the wash cycle to help clean your laundry in place of laundry detergent.

- There are also plenty of other frugal uses for lemon around the house.

Borax

Borax is a great all-around cleaner, disinfectant, and deodorizer. Borax can be used to remove stains on floors, walls, ceilings, and counters. You can also make it into a powerful paste that you can use to scrub, rinse, and wipe clean. Consider just a few uses for Borax around the house:

- Borax is a great drain cleaner. It sanitizes the garbage disposal, eliminates pests, and gets rid of the decaying sink smell.

- Borax is also a great toilet cleaner when mixed with water.

- Use Borax to clean garbage cans to reduce odors in the home.

- It is also a great carpet stain remover that also deodorizes. Mix with water and spray or apply to the stain.

- A tablespoon of Borax added in the dishwasher will help remove water spots.

- There are also ample other uses for Borax around the house to help you save money.

Witch Hazel

In addition to cleaning, this is a great item to have on hand because it can also offer great beauty benefits. Consider some of the ways it can be used in cleaning.

- Baking soda and witch hazel can be combined for a great bathroom cleaner. You won't have harmful chemicals, and you'll have a clean bathroom.

- Witch hazel is also a great floor cleaner; just mix a small amount with warm water.

- Witch hazel is also a great glass cleaner in the home and your car as well.

- There are also a number of beauty, and other household uses as well.

Baking Soda

Baking soda has long been used as an effective and natural cleaning agent. You can use water to make it into a paste to clean counters, tile, and floors. We'll discuss the main uses for baking soda shortly.

Vinegar

While having a strong smell, vinegar is a great way to degrease. You can also use it to remove mildew in the bathroom and leaves no streaks on windows. Apply vinegar, allow it to sit, and then scrub to clean. It can also be used in the wash for mildewed towels in order to get rid of the odor. We'll discuss more vinegar and its cleaning properties soon.

Cornstarch

In addition to being a great depression-era addition to recipes, cornstarch is also a great cleaning agent. Consider just a few of the cleaning options available:

- Cornstarch is a great carpet cleaner. Sprinkle it on stains and allow it to sit for twenty minutes. Scrub lightly with a brush and then vacuum.

- It is also a great absorber for stains like salt, but will also help get rid of odors.

Soap

A great natural cleanser for the home is basic liquid soap. There are a few great options for this:

- Add a tablespoon to warm mop water, and it can help with scrubbing sinks and tubs.

- A tablespoon of soap with a gallon of warm water can make a great floor cleaner.

- Liquid dish soap can also be used to wash laundry.

Alcohol

Isopropyl is a great cleaner around the home. It is also great for disinfecting surfaces. Use it to clean counters, sinks, tubs, and anywhere that germs are likely.

Now let's look closer at three of the most common household cleaning products and how they can save you money on cleaning your home: vinegar, baking soda, and borax.

Cleaning with Vinegar

Vinegar is one of the best cleaning agents you need to start using in your home. It is a power disinfectant that can be easily purchased in bulk for cheap. It has been shown that vinegar can kill E.coli, Salmonella, and Staphylococcus. It is also a natural and safe cleaner. Using vinegar to clean your home can save you hundreds a year on cleaning supplies. As you start using vinegar to clean the home, consider the following ways you can use vinegar to clean your home.

- **Rid Your Pantry of Small Critters.** At some point, you are likely going to find critters in your pantry. If you're trying to store up a depression-era pantry, this is something you don't want to have happen. Pour one and a half cups of apple cider vinegar in a cup with two drops of original Dawn. Leave uncovered in the pantry for about a week to attract bugs. To prevent infestation, toss anything destroyed and wash the shelves with Dawn.

- **Floor Cleaning.** A 50/50 vinegar and water solution can be used to clean tile or linoleum floors. You won't get the suds as you see with soap, but you will have clean and sanitized floors.

- **Mirror Cleaning.** A mix of ¼ cup vinegar to ¾ cup rubbing alcohol can make a great cleaner for windows that leaves no streaks behind. Spray the mix on the mirror and then wipe with a lint-free cloth. It is a great way to disinfect mirrors in the bathroom.

- **Odor Remover.** If you have smells in your home, you can remove them by setting a few bowls of vinegar in different places. The vinegar soaks up smells in a day or two. Add a few separate bowls with baking soda or pour vinegar undiluted onto a rag and wave around the room to speed up the deodorizing process.

- **Clean Computer Accessories.** A Q-tip dipped in vinegar is a great way to clean out all the nooks in your keyboard or monitor. Never spray it directly on electronics and make sure you don't reach electrical currents with the swab; otherwise, you could short them out and ruin your electronics.

- **Remove Ink.** Spraying undiluted vinegar on an ink stain and letting it sit for five minutes before wiping clean will easily remove ink stains.

- **Clean Blinds.** The blinds in your windows are an extremely hard area to clean, but with a 50/50 mixture of vinegar and hot water will make this a much easier task. Spray a light mist and then use a lint-free cloth to wipe clean.

- **Kitchen Degreaser.** Kitchens are messy and usually end up with a layer of grease. Mix 50/50 vinegar with water, spray directly on the surface and then wipe off for a powerful degreaser. You can also add your favorite scent in the form of essential oils if you want a little better smell and remember to completely mix the oils by shaking before each use.

- **Carpet Shampoo.** Use a mixture of one cup vinegar to a gallon of water in a carpet shampooer. You won't have to worry about fading your carpets, using hard chemicals and you'll deodorize your carpet.

- **Mildew Prevention.** If you have outdoor furniture or fabric in your home that you are concerned about a mildew smell, spray it down with full-strength vinegar. Spray with a light mist, so you don't cause additional issues, and you'll be able to prevent mildew growth.

- **Leather Cleaner.** Mixing vinegar with boiled linseed oil is a great leather cleaner. Spray as a light mist and then wipe off with a soft cloth.

- **Wood Scratch Repair.** Apple cider vinegar mixed with iodine in equal parts can be painted on wood scratches. It will repair the scratch and have your wood looking like new. If the wood is darker, you can always add more iodine.

- **Removed Melted Wax.** Equal parts vinegar and water can be used to remove melted wax. Start by blow-drying the wax and removing what you can, then clean the rest up with the vinegar mixture, and you should be able to remove it completely.

- **Toilet Cleaner and Disinfectant.** Put a half cup baking soda into your toilet bowl and clean with a toilet brush. Then add one cup of vinegar. After the foaming action has stopped, flush to clean and disinfect your toilet. If you simply want to disinfect, then pour in the vinegar and swish around; allow to sit for five minutes and then flush.

- **Polish Features.** If your faucet and other bathroom fixtures look a little dull? Spray on full strength vinegar and wipe clean; metal surfaces will start to shine.

- **Unclog Drains.** Pour a half-cup baking soda down the drain and follow with one cup of vinegar. Allow it to sit until the foaming stops. Rinse the drain with a cup of hot water and then free-flowing cold water. This should free up the drain, and it will also have the added benefit of removing odors.

- **Stainless Steel Cleaner.** You don't need to buy special stainless steel cleaners as long as you have vinegar. Spray a light mist on the surface and wipe with a lint-free cloth to remove things like fingerprints.

- **Oven and Microwave Cleaner.** At some point, the microwave is going to need a thorough cleaning. Vinegar can make the toughest messes easier. Mix ¼ cup water with one cup vinegar and add to a microwave-safe bowl. Microwave on high for two to three minutes to make the grime easier to remove. It should wipe off completely. Add ¼ of a lemon to the mix if you want to make it smell clean and add a little shine.

- **Refrigerator Cleaner.** A 50/50 mix of vinegar and water can be used to clean out your refrigerator. It removes dirt, disinfects, and prevents "growth" on food that may be kept in there a little too long. Plus, it will help clean out any lingering odors.

☐ **Clean and Disinfect Cutting Boards.** Wooden cutting boards can be difficult to clean without help from vinegar. Sprinkle baking soda on the board and then lightly spray with full-strength vinegar. Once the foam has dried, you can rinse with cold water. Allow it to dry completely before using or putting away somewhere. This method works well for cleaning both wood and plastic cutting boards.

☐ **Coffee Pot Cleaner.** Over time the coffee pot can be very grimy. Add full-strength vinegar to the water reservoir and run a complete cycle. Follow by running a cycle of water through the pot until the vinegar smell is gone. It can take several cycles of water to remove all the residue of vinegar, but once it does, you'll have a like-new coffee pot.

Cleaning with Baking Soda

There are lots of ways to use baking soda to clean your home, and a box of it is cheap enough to reduce your monthly budget for cleaning supplies. Baking soda is a mild abrasive that can be used to clean in the kitchen, bathroom, and nearly everywhere else in the house. Let's look at some of the areas in your house and techniques for cleaning with baking soda.

Kitchen

- **Sink.** Make a paste from baking soda and water. Rub the paste on the sink and allow it to sit briefly before rubbing it in a little and then rinsing well. This will clean your sink and also leave it with a light and fresh scent.

- **Stove.** Combine one part baking soda, one part water, and one part table salt into a paste. Using a damp rag, scrub the top of the stove, and wipe clean. You'll get rid of stuck-on food, grease, and grime in no time.

- **Microwave.** Mix four tablespoons of baking soda with a quart of water and use it to wipe down the inside of the microwave in order to get rid of grime and dirt. It can also remove odors of food from the microwave.

- **Refrigerator.** Keeping a box of baking soda in the refrigerator can help absorb odors and keep things smelling fresh. However, you can also mix a little baking soda with vinegar to produce a bubbly mixture that can be used to wipe down the walls and shelves of the refrigerator.

- **Dishwasher.** Pour a cup of baking soda into the dishwasher and run it through a cycle without any dishes. This will help remove detergent build-up. It is best to do it about once a month to keep grime to a minimum.

- **Counters.** Sprinkle baking soda on the counter and wipe clean with a damp rag. If there are stains, you can make a paste with baking soda and water; allow it to sit on the stain for about fifteen minutes before scrubbing thoroughly and then rinsing clean.

Bathroom

- **Bathtub.** Fill a spray bottle with vinegar and spray down the sides and bottom of the bathtub. Then sprinkle baking soda over the vinegar. Allow it to sit for a few minutes, then scrub with a rag or sponge. You'll remove all the built-up grime.

- **Sink.** Pour one cup of baking soda down the drain and follow it with one cup of very hot water. Allow five minutes for the mix to start working and then follow with a gallon of very hot water. Depending on your bathroom sink, you may have to do this a few times, but eventually, all the clogs of hair and grime will be cleared. You can also do it every couple of weeks for routine maintenance and keeping your pipes from clogging.

- **Hairbrush.** Make a solution of baking soda and water to soak your hairbrushes. Allow to soak for about thirty minutes and then rinse well.

Other Cleaning Uses

- **Flooring.** Mix a ½ cup baking soda in a warm bucket of soapy water. Mop the floor and then rinse well.

- **Litter Boxes.** A cat litter box can easily build up odors, even if it is cleaned every day. Sprinkle baking soda inside the box every few days in order to keep it from smelling.

- **Carpeting.** Sprinkling baking soda throughout the house on the carpet and allowing it to sit for thirty minutes or so and then vacuum to remove odors.

- **Scuff Marks.** Sprinkle baking soda on the scuff marks and scrub with a damp cloth or sponge. You'll easily remove the scuff marks, and your floor will look like new again.

- **Trash Cans.** Sprinkle baking soda in the bottom of your trash gains in order to keep odors from building up and smelling up your home.

- **Garage.** Baking soda is a great option for absorbing grease spills.

- **Shoes.** You can even sprinkle baking soda inside shoes and allow it to sit overnight. This will help reduce smelly shoes and feet.

There are plenty of ways to use baking soda throughout your home, not just in cleaning. It is a great product to purchase and have on hand for its great number of uses.

Cleaning with Borax

Borax is commonly known as a laundry booster, but it can be used for a number of other household cleaning uses. It is a natural mineral and a very eco-friendly household cleaner. However, it shouldn't be ingested, so you should use caution if using it around children and pets. Let's look at some of the cleanings uses for Borax.

- Sprinkle an equal mix of Borax and sugar in order to keep roaches and ants out of your home.

- Wash outdoor furniture with a mix of 1 teaspoon dish detergent, 1 teaspoon borax, and 1-quart warm water; this will help clean off mildew.

- Put 3 tablespoons of Borax in your garbage disposal and allow it to sit for an hour before flushing with warm water. This will get rid of odors while sanitizing and cleaning your garbage disposal.

- Use a mix of 1 teaspoon of Borax and warm water to scrub dirty pots and pans. Since Borax is non-abrasive, it will break down grime without damaging surface material.

- Mix 2 tablespoons Borax and 2 cups hot water in a spray bottle for an all-purpose cleaner.

- Mix ¼ cup Borax and 1 cup water for use as a carpet stain remover and deodorizer. Spray or pour directly on the stain.

- You can use Borax and lemon juice to make a paste to scrub and remove rust. After just rinse and pat dry.

- One tablespoon of Borax added to the dishwasher will help remove water spots from your dishes.

- Add 1 cup Borax and 2 cups water in order to glean out garbage cans.

- Add ¼ to ½ cup Borax to the toilet bowl and scrub with a brush before flushing to rinse clean.

These are some great general uses for cleaning your home. Another aspect of keeping your home clean is to keep it organized. There are some depression-era tips that can help you in this endeavor as well.

Depression-era Life Hacks for Organization and Storage

Organizing your home can certainly make life easier, but not many know it can also save you a lot of money. An organized home will keep your finances in a better balance. Before we get into how to organize your home, let's take a moment to consider just how you can save money with home organization.

In addition to saving money, organization can also help you make money. You can sell items that you find you're not using. You may find out you have a very valuable item that is simply gathering dust. Even if you don't sell items, you may be able to get a tax break at the end of the year if you donate your items.

Organization is key to becoming less wasteful. This is especially true when it comes to organizing your food pantry. When you know what you have in your kitchen, you'll be less likely to forget about something. This means food is less likely to expire, and you'll have more options when it comes to making your meals.

As soon as you start to organize, you'll be amazed at how much "stuff" you have. It can be overwhelming at first, but it will also prevent you from going out and purchasing more. It will help you better evaluate things when you want to make a purchase.

An organized home will also mean you won't forget about things like gift cards, small checks, and other items that are basically the same as money sitting around your home. When you are organized, you'll be able to keep track of these things and use them before they expire.

Organization also means you'll be able to keep track of your bills and won't be faced with late fees. Knowing when things are due with organization will make paying the bills smoother because you won't forget things.

If you are building a pantry to ensure you are prepared for a depression, then you're likely developing a stockpile. You should keep this stockpile organized in order to know what you need and what is getting low. If it isn't organized, you could end up buying too much of something and have no room to store it.

So how do you go about getting organized and doing it in a frugal way? Let's look at two main ways to save money when organizing: repurposed items and the dollar store.

Repurposed Organization

It's always a good idea to start thinking about spring cleaning and organizing. Despite a lot of the advertisements and ads, you don't need to spend a lot of money on organizing tools and storage containers. You probably already have all you need to organize at home. The following are some general ideas for common items you can repurpose into organizers for your home. There are plenty more options available to you, but this is to help get you started. Take a look around your home and think about how you can repurpose items for your organizational needs.

Cocoa Cans/Containers

If you use cocoa either for baking or hot chocolate, once you're finished, be sure to save the can/container. You can never have enough of these. Often packaged goods come in containers that are made from good quality materials and can easily serve another function. Cover the container with paper and make your own design or label for a variety of uses around the home.

Wine Crates

Not everyone has wine crates lying around the house. However, if you have an organizing project that would benefit from these, you can always ask your local grocery or liquor store to set some aside for you. You can even put these crates together to create storage carts.

Empty Bottles

Perhaps the one area in the home that has the most odds and

ends floating around is the bathroom. There are razors, bar soaps, toys, etc. Clean up and organize this space by using empty shampoo bottles to serve as containers for the smaller items in the area.

There are plenty of ways to organize your home, and if you take a moment to consider what your needs are, you'll likely find something to repurpose in your own home. So before you go to the store, take the time to consider what you need to organize and whether or not you have a container in your home. If you do need to purchase containers, you can save money by going to the dollar store for your shopping.

Dollar Store Organization

Reducing clutter and organizing are great ways to save time and money while also getting your living space to look much better. We've already discussed how you can repurpose items in your home, but maybe you don't have all the storage containers you need. If this is the case, you can still organize your home on a very limited budget. Just head to your local Dollar Store, where you can find all the storage containers you need for a fraction of the cost. Let's look at how you can organize your home for less.

The first step is to clean and purge as much stuff as you can. Save only items that are useful and fits in with your current lifestyle. Once you've paired things down to a minimalist lifestyle, then you can get started on organizing everything. When it comes to organizing, the most important thing is to use containers that you can see through and allow you to organize items in a way you can see them at a glance. Consider how you can organize various areas in your home.

Kitchen

Using containers in your kitchen is a great way to organize individual packages of food such as oatmeal packets, granola bars, etc. Use the same size and color containers on each shelf for a more uniformed and organized look. When you don't have boxes falling and items stacked on top of each other, then you'll have less food waste, and you won't waste money buying things you already have.

You can also use containers in the refrigerator. A basket can hold small snacks, juice boxes, or fruits and vegetables. You won't have to spend a lot, and you'll be able to see everything better.

If you don't have a spice rack, consider a small shallow bin that can hold your spices in a cupboard near your stove for quick and easy access while cooking.

Small shallow containers can also be used to organize drawers. Have a container for all small items such as cords, batteries, and pens. You can also organize your condiments and small kitchen gadgets.

Bathroom

There is plenty of space for containers in the bathroom: back of the toilet, under the sink, in drawers, on shelves, or in a linen closet. Organize your small items like travel toiletries, hair ties, makeup, and all other small-sized items. A basket with a handle is great for organizing cleaning supplies under the bathroom sink. Organizing your washcloths by rolling them and keeping them in a basket.

Bedroom

Containers can be used in drawers to separate and organize socks and underwear. A small container on your side table can hold change, keys, and other items you empty from your pockets. Larger bins can be added to the closet to store seasonal items like hats and scarves. You can also do similar organizing with under the bed organizers.

Laundry Room

A small basic is a great place to keep hand wash items separate from regular laundry. A bin for laundry soap, fabric softener, and stain removal helps keep things organized and easier to clean if there is a leak. Small jars can be used to organize small items like clothespins and wool dryer balls.

The possibilities are clearly endless when it comes to organizing your home. Start with containers you already have and then make a list of what you still need to organize and what types of containers you'll likely need. Then head to the Dollar Store and buy what you think you need; you can always return and exchange if you need different sizes or purchase more than you need. For a small investment at a dollar store, you can make a big difference in the organization of your home.

Once you have things organized, you can also start to look for ways that you can budget and save money within your own home. Let's now look at some depression-era tips that can help you save money on household expenses.

Depression-era Household Management Life Hacks

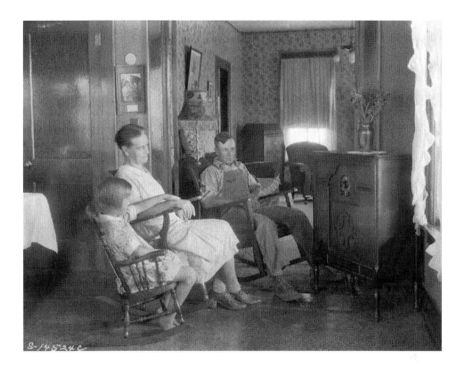

When it comes to saving money on household expenses, the most important thing to do is set a schedule. Focus on one main task each day so you can eliminate using things like electricity too much. It will also leave you more time for things like meal planning and cooking. You may have something like the following:

- ☐ Laundry on Monday

- ☐ Ironing on Tuesday

- ☐ Mending on Wednesday

- ☐ Cleaning on Thursday

- ☐ Shopping on Friday

- ☐ Cooking on Saturday

- ☐ Resting on Sunday

A schedule gives you a framework for getting bigger tasks done along with all the smaller daily chores you need to accomplish. It also makes things more efficient. Let's consider how you can reduce the cost of household expenses.

Cutting Household Expenses

During the Great Depression, they didn't have nearly as many monthly expenses as we do now. Yet the principle they applied then still applies today; if you don't need it, you shouldn't be paying for it. Take a look at your monthly expenses and see what you can cut. Even if you use it every day, is it a luxury that you can't really afford to keep going? There are a number of reasons to make cuts, and it can be overwhelming to decide what to get rid of. However, you can make a huge difference to your finances by making the right cuts to household expenses. Let's consider eleven of the most common areas where you can cut household expenses and see if any apply to you.

Cable

When it comes to watching television, there are lots of options today. You don't need to keep paying a high cable bill. Rather consider how much you watch television and what channels you view; it may be less expensive to use a digital service or another alternative to cable. Just make sure you don't end up paying more for streaming services than you did on cable. Consider your needs and determine what is best for your situation.

Credit Cards

Interest charges on credit cards can have a big enough impact on your budget. However, if you have a card with an annual fee, then this is one of the first expenses you should attempt to cut. If possible, move the balance to another card with a lower interest rate and no fee. Close any accounts that have annual fees.

Housekeeping

Most people may not use these services, but if you do, then evaluate why you have it. If you legitimately need the assistance of keeping your house in order, then you may want to continue. However, if you have a housekeeper or maid service simply because you feel you don't have the time to do it yourself, then you may need to do a little evaluation. Make a monthly calendar and assign a few cleaning tasks a day or week, depending on your schedule. If you can complete these tasks yourself, then you'll save money while also giving yourself a sense of accomplishment.

Meal Delivery

Meal subscription boxes are fun and convenient. Having food delivered from a restaurant is convenient after a long day of work. But can you do the same on your own with a few simple ingredients or with items you currently have stocked in your pantry? If you need it, you can still purchase prepared meals from the grocery store until you are able to budget your time for your own cooking.

Electrical Usage

With a little effort, it is possible for you to lower your electric bill. Ensure you have energy-efficient light bulbs and appliances, if possible. Set up automated timers to shut off lights and electronics when you aren't using them. Unplug items when you aren't using them. Best of all, keep your family aware of how much electricity is used each month. Everything helps. We'll look a little closer at this area later when we discuss ways to save on your utilities.

Water Use

You can also save money by reducing how much water you use. Put a timer in the bathroom so you can monitor how long your showers are and you can practice showering with less water. Ensure all leaks are fixed in your pipes. Wash clothes and dishes only when there is a full load. These are just a few simple ways to reduce your water bill.

Lawn Care

Paying someone to care for your lawn adds up, and it can also impact your water bill as well. There are plenty of tutorials online to help you do your own lawn care, plus you can install landscaping that is less work and uses less water. If you don't have all the equipment, you need you can consider borrowing from a neighbor or renting only when you need it.

Newspaper or Magazine Subscriptions

Nearly everything is available online today, so paying for newspaper or magazine subscriptions is something you may not need. Going paperless will not only save you money but will also reduce paper waste. If you still prefer to hold a physical copy, then consider borrowing from the local library.

Paper Products

As with newspapers and magazines, if you can go paperless in as many ways as possible, this will help reduce household expenses. Consider reducing your use of paper products like paper towels, plastic bags, and napkins. When you use reusable versions, you'll save money while also reducing waste.

Landline Phone

If you still have a landline phone take the time to consider the pros and cons to evaluate if you really need one. Cell phone plans are becoming cheaper, and many are getting rid of landline phones. If you feel you still need a landline, then do some comparison shopping to make sure you get the cheapest possible plan.

Memberships and Subscriptions

Periodically you should look through your memberships and subscriptions to see which ones you aren't using. Is there something set up on autopay that you've forgotten about? Canceling unused items may not seem like a lot, but it can add up to significant savings at the end of the year.

Cutting your household expenses is one of the best ways to prepare for a depression and start setting aside money. Look at these options and see which ones can help you. Perhaps one area where we can all save is by reducing the cost of our utilities. Let's look more closely at how you can save on your electric bill.

Saving on Your Electric Bill

In recent years, electric rates have continued to climb. This can easily have an impact on your monthly budget. There are ways you can help lower your electric bill and live more frugally, even in the hotter summer months.

Talk with Your Electric Company

If you notice your rates increasing, the first thing you should do is call your electric company and ask them if there are any programs you and your household qualify for. You'll have to answer a series of questions in order to determine if you may qualify for programs. If you don't qualify for any programs, you can ask about averaging your electric bill, so you are able to pay a single flat rate each month. This will at least save you a little each month.

Turn Off Lights

While this may sound like an obvious solution, it's also easy to forget to turn off lights when you leave a room. Start making it your habit to turn off lights whenever you're not in a room. When you go to bed, make sure all outdoor lights are off as well. If needed, you can set up motion lighting outside.

Avoid the Dryer

If possible, you should hang your clothes out to dry. Running a dryer, especially for those with a lot of laundry, can easily increase the monthly electricity bill. Using a simple clothesline is a great way to save on your monthly bills.

Set up a Charging Station

If you have electronics plugged in all over the house to charge, it can waste a lot of power. Rather you should consider setting up a central location with a power surge protector and then all the chargers. If something is not being charged, you should turn the surge protector off. While this may only save you a few dollars a month, it can still add up to significant savings at the end of the year.

Better Light Bulbs

Traditional and cheaper light bulbs are actually more expensive to run. It is better to pay the higher price upfront for compact fluorescent light bulbs and save money on their monthly usage.

Reduce TV Time

Some family households can have three or more TVs on at the same time. This can cost a lot of money. Start by turning off the TV during dinner, when the phone rings, during homework hours, and when you go to bed. On the weekends, you can even set time limits for watching TV to help reduce electricity usage.

Regular Household Maintenance

It is important to make sure all major appliances are up to date and that the heating and A/C are in working order to keep your monthly electric bill low. Outdated appliances can sometimes be replaced with a rebate from the utility company if you need to buy new energy-efficient appliances.

Programmable Thermostats

Using a programmable thermostat with your heater or A/C means they will only run when you want them to. Often this only costs about thirty dollars, and you may even be able to get one for free from your electric company.

Switch to Solar

If you choose to switch to solar power, then it is important to note you won't start saving money right away. Often the long-term savings can be worth the cost of switching to solar. You'll also be able to find rebate programs to help lower the cost of switching to solar.

Get the Most Out of Cooking Time

This is where meal planning can help. You should avoid preheating the oven if possible. It is also a good idea to cook several meals at a time to limit the number of times you have to heat the oven.

In addition to these tips, it can be a good idea to look into ways to cool down without air conditioning. The cost of running an air conditioning unit in the summer can cause the electricity bill to skyrocket. Let's consider how you can cool your home without air conditioning.

Cooling without Air Conditioning

In the summer months, the temperature can reach up to triple-digit temperatures. Trying to have a cool home while also managing a lower electric bill isn't that easy. However, there are ways that you can keep your home cool without using an air conditioner and raising the cost of your electricity bill.

Follow the Weather

The weather forecast can be accessed from a variety of sources today: television, smartphones, and the internet. Use these resources to follow the weather. If the temperatures are going to drop overnight, then you should keep your windows open. If you see a heatwave starting, then start to cool down your home in advance by closing drapes and keeping fans running.

Close the Drapes

When the drapes or other window coverings are open, the sunlight comes inside. If the temperature reaches the triple digits, then the sunlight can easily heat up your home. Keep your window coverings closed in order to keep your home cool. You may even want to consider investing in blackout curtains to significantly decrease the amount of sunlight that comes inside your home.

Use Ceiling Fans

Ceiling fans can be a great investment and not just for the summer months. During the winter, you can also use a ceiling fan to push hot air down from the ceiling. Ceiling fans can often be very affordable to purchase, and they are easy to install.

Plant Trees

If there isn't a lot of shade around your home, you should consider making some by planting trees. Trees and shrubbery are a great way to keep your home shaded. Some electric companies will even offer trees for free to customers.

Don't Use the Oven

In the summer months, using the oven will quickly make the temperature rise in your home. Rather than use your oven, consider meals that don't need to be cooked or use other methods such as the crockpot. Another great choice is to use a barbecue outdoors.

Speak with the Professionals

Have a professional come inspect your home to see if you have anything making your home warmer. Sometimes this service can be offered through the electric company, or you can speak with a local A/C company. A simple inspection can often save you hundreds of dollars a year.

These are general ways to save on household expenses. A more specific thing to consider is your household appliances. Not only do you want to save money when purchasing and using household appliances, but you also want to get as much life out of your appliances as possible. First, we will consider what uses you can get from a household appliance, and then we'll consider which kitchen appliances are best to purchase second hand to save you additional funds.

Household Appliances

Many households have common kitchen appliances like a coffee maker, dishwasher, microwave, etc. These appliances make life much more convenient than it was during the Great Depression. Yet, most people don't realize you can use these items for more than their intended purposes, so you can get more for your money. Consider some of the ways you can use your appliances that you likely never thought of before.

Coffee Pot

A coffee pot can be for pretty much anything that needs hot water without having to use the stove. It can be a great way to heat water for your morning oatmeal or hot chocolate. It doesn't just have to be for coffee.

Food Processor or Blender

A food processor can be a great way to make pizza dough for dinner or for homemade peanut butter. Simply puree peanuts with a bit of honey to taste until you get the desired consistency.

Microwave

The microwave can be used to sanitize the kitchen sponge by placing it damp in the microwave and zapping for 30 seconds. The microwave can also make juicing citrus fruits easier. Microwave lemons and limes for fifteen seconds, and getting the juice out will be much easier.

Slow Cooker or Crock Pot

The low or warm setting on a crockpot can proof your bread. You can also use it to make your own soap or use it as a fondue pot.

Dishwasher

The dishwasher can be used to clean so much more than dishes. Use it to clean baseball hats, refrigerator shelves, produce drawers, and pretty much any other item. It will save you a lot of time by not having to scrub by hand; just stick it in for a cycle.

Waffle Maker

You can use this to make a complete breakfast for one person. Put some bacon on one half and hash browns on the other, and you'll have a great breakfast in no time.

Stand Mixer

Many people don't know you can use this to shred the meat for dinner recipes. Place cooked and slightly broken up meat on a low setting with the beaters. This will save you a lot of time shredding by hand for dinners. It is also a great way to make whipped butter.

Rice Cooker

You can cook a lot more than rice. Think of it as a small crockpot that can be used to cook things like oatmeal. You can also poach fruit like pears or apples to make a wonderful dessert.

Immersion Blender

Any meal you eat can be made into baby food by placing some in a pot and adding a little liquid before blending to a puree. This will make it easier for people with children to make their own baby food, which can be pretty expensive if you buy it in the store.

Coffee Grinder

The coffee grinder is a great way that you can mince herbs. It can also be a quick way to chop nuts for recipes that require small pieces.

Now that you know the many uses kitchen appliances can

have, you'll see why it is important to have them around. However, in order to truly get your money's worth for them, you should learn which ones to purchase second hand.

Kitchen Gadgets Second Hand

The cost of furnishing a kitchen can be a bit costly, but with so much use, you can get out of certain items; it is good to keep them on hand. Thankfully, there are many kitchen items that are fine to purchase used. Consider the following items that you can buy used at a thrift store to save money when furnishing your kitchen.

Mixing Bowls

Quality mixing bowls are very durable, easy to clean, and often are oven and dishwasher safe. Rather than spending a lot of money on a set of your own, look for a set at yard sales and thrift stores. Find ones that are glass in various sizes and check the bottom to ensure they are oven and dishwasher safe. Avoid bowls that are chipped or cracked since they can harbor bacteria.

Cast Iron Cookware

Cast iron pots and pans are great for sautéing and stovetop cooking. When you find one, you only need to clean and season it to make it as good as new. If you can find them in a variety of sizes, you'll be able to use them for all of your cooking needs.

Measuring Cups

It is a good idea to collect an assortment of measuring cups in a variety of sizes, so you'll always have them available when cooking. Having a few extra on hand is good in case one gets lost or broken. You often can find these for under a dollar at thrift stores, so you'll be able to get a complete set for cheap.

Timers

Kitchen timers are great for a variety of tasks. A new one isn't that expensive, but you can save even more money by getting one used. Even if you have one, you should have a backup if the price is right.

Tablecloths

A seasonal tablecloth is a great way to dress up your table. It'll light up a room and make guests feel special. New tablecloths cost more than you may think, so finding a used one can be a great option. Use lemon juice to remove any stains, and they'll look like new.

Aprons

If you like to wear an apron while cooking, you know how quickly they can get dirty. Rather than paying the price for a new one, purchase a used one. You can often wash out stains if needed.

Drink Pitchers

These are great to have when making drink mixes or having guests over for a drink. Buy a quality glass one at a thrift store. After a good cleaning, you are ready to go, and you'll be saving a hefty amount on the price.

Mini Grills

You will often find these at yard sales and thrift stores. When buying new, these can be quite expensive, and you can save a lot of money buying one used. These used to be popular and can still be used, but the value has gone down, and many people don't need them anymore.

Serving Pieces

If you entertain guests often, you should look at thrift stores for serving pieces. You'll often find everything you need to entertain for far less than buying all the items new. Often you'll get an entire set for the same price as a single new item.

Canisters

Canisters are a great way to store bulk items like coffee, tea, sugar, and other dry goods. Buying a set of canisters from a thrift store or a garage salc is a great option. You can either look for a matching set or create your own unique set from different canisters.

While there are a lot of kitchen items you should buy new, there are also plenty of things you can buy used. Keep these in mind when you plan to furnish a kitchen. Another way to save on household expenses is to reduce paper products in the kitchen and elsewhere in the house.

Reducing Paper Products

In addition to saving money, you are also saving the environment when you choose to reduce the number of paper products you use. There are five main ways that you can use cloth rather than paper products, and they are easy to implement. While you'll have to do a little more laundry, it won't have any major difference in the cost of purchasing paper products.

Hand Towels vs. Paper Towels

Rather than buy a roll of paper towels for your bathroom or kitchen, you can use cloth hand towels. Each family member can have their own towel in the bathroom. When you hang them to dry, they won't harbor mold or germs, and if you only use them to dry your hands, there won't be cross-contamination.

Cloth Napkins vs. Paper Napkins

This is possibly one of the easiest changes to do. Buy a set of cloth napkins to use at mealtimes. If you need a larger amount, you can save money by purchasing bandannas at a craft store or discount store. This is a frugal, function, and convenient way to reduce your use of paper napkins.

Cloth Diapers vs. Regular Diapers

If you have children, this can take a bit getting used to, and it can be an investment at first. However, it is a great way to stay eco-friendly while also stretching your budget. Disposable diapers and baby wipes as well can add up on the budget. Using cloth diapers and line drying them can save you a lot of money.

Cloth Feminine Hygiene Products vs. Traditional Products

This can be a great natural choice, and there are plenty of options to choose from. Most are made with similar fabrics and inserts similar to cloth diapers. The products are easy to use, wash, and reuse just like a cloth diaper, but without the bulk. This is also a great way to avoid the use of chemicals.

Cleaning Cloths vs. Paper Towels

When it comes to wiping down surfaces and cleaning places

around the house, you can choose from a variety of reusable options. You can purchase shop towels or use old sheets and blankets cut apart. No matter what type of cloth you use, you will reduce waste and upcycle items in your home to save money.

With just a few minor adjustments, you can easily switch from using disposable paper products to reusable options. Doing this on a regular basis is going to save money on your monthly budget while helping the environment.

Depression-era Healthcare and Beauty Hacks

Depression-era Healthcare Hacks

Modern science and medicine have done a lot for people, and it continues to make our lives better. However, during the Great Depression, our relatives often relied on ingenuity and thriftiness to keep themselves well. For non-emergency situations, consider trying the Great Depression health hacks.

Bites

For things like bug bites and bee stings, you can mix some baking soda with water to make a paste. Apply the paste over the bite and allow it to sit. After it dried, the baking soda flakes off, and you can apply more paste.

Upset Stomach

Comfrey tea can help ease a number of ailments, but it is typically used for upset stomachs. Steep some tea and then enjoy a drink. You can buy the tea in stores or grow your own.

Fever

It may sound weird, but placing whole slices of fresh onion on the bottom of your feet can help with a fever. Slip tight-fitting socks over the onions and then gently massage to help your body absorb them quicker. If possible, replace every four to six hours and continue as long as you have a fever.

Splinters

If you find yourself with a splinter stuck in your skin, this trick is going to help remove it. Remove a piece of the thin, white membrane from the inside of a freshly cracked egg. Cover the splinter site with this membrane-like a band-aid overnight, and the splinter will come to the surface.

Colds and Flu

With the cold and flu season getting longer each year, it can be a good idea to have vapor rub on hand. Save money by making your own and having it available whenever you need it.

Ingredients:

- [ ] 20 drops Eucalyptus essential oil

- [ ] 15 drops Peppermint essential oil

- [ ] 4 tablespoons shea butter

- [ ] 2 and ½ tablespoons coconut oil

- [ ] 4-ounce mason jar with a lid or sealable glass container

Directions:

- [ ] Fill a small saucepan ⅓ full with water and place over medium/low heat.

- [ ] Place the jar in the water without getting water into the jar.

- [ ] Add shea butter to the jar.

- [ ] Once melted, add the coconut oil and stir to combine.

- [ ] Once both are melted, remove the jar from the saucepan.

- [ ] Allow the mixture to cool to room temperature or about fifteen minutes.

☐ Add the essential oils and stir again.

☐ Allow to cool until solid, then seal with the lid.

☐ Store in a cool, dry place, and it will be good for up to a year.

Depression-era Beauty Hacks

Women of the Depression-era were pioneers of the frugal living movement. Compromises were made to avoid spending money on luxuries such as makeup. As a result, many of the women of that era found beauty hacks with everyday items that they had on hand. You can find these tips helpful today to help you save money.

- Wash and condition your hair with a tablespoon baking soda. Simply rub into wet hair and then rinse well. You can also condition your hair with a bit of raw egg yolk and rinse with cool water.

- Keep your brows in place with a bit of olive oil or Vaseline, depending on your preference.

- Witch hazel can help with under-eye puffiness. Dab a bit under each eye with a cotton ball and avoid getting it into your eyes. You can also use a bit of petroleum jelly each night for the same effect.

- Exfoliate your skin with salt or sugar scrubs.

- A bit of baking soda and coconut oil can make a cheap and effective toothpaste.

These are just a couple of the general beauty tips you can learn from women of the depression-era. There are three main ingredients that have wide use in the health and beauty hacks from the Great Depression-era: Tea Tree Oil, Coconut Oil, and Witch Hazel. Having these on hand means you can do a lot for your health and beauty on a budget. Let's look at what each of these can do.

Uses for Tea Tree Oil

Tea tree oil is simple and yet very effective when it comes to treating ailments and making life better in a variety of ways. Consider the following areas where depression-era people learned to used tea tree oil.

1. One drop of oil with a teaspoon of water makes a mouthwash. Rinse and spit well, avoid swallowing.

2. Two tablespoons of tea tree oil added to bathwater can help with body aches.

3. A few drops on a cotton ball and gently dabbed on blisters once a day will soothe them and help them go away.

4. Add a few drops to a warm, damp washcloth and place on the chest for ten to fifteen minutes to help ease chest congestion.

5. A drop of oil rubbed on dry and cracked lips will give instant relief to chapped lips.

6. Apply a paste of cornstarch and tea tree oil to the chickenpox affected area to treat and dry the area.

7. Add a few drops of tea tree oil into a vaporizer to get relief from the worst coughs.

8. Adding seven to ten drops of tea tree oil to your shampoo will help stimulate the scalp and get rid of dandruff.

9. Reduce the symptoms of an ear infection when you apply two drops of tea tree oil with one teaspoon of olive oil into the ear. Absorb the oil after two minutes using a dry swab.

10. A dab of tea tree oil to flea bites can lessen the itch and increase healing. It also works well for other insect bites like mosquito bites.

11. Tea tree oil can be used to clean hairbrushes and toothbrushes by soaking in a gallon of hot water and a

few drops of tea tree oil. Soak, rinse, and repeat as needed.

12. Tea tree oil on a cotton ball can be rubbed gently on acne affected areas. It will soothe the skin and lessen redness while promoting healing.

13. Soaking your feet in hot water with a few teaspoons of tea tree oil will help reduce the athlete's foot. Dry and repeat as needed.

14. Massage tea tree oil into the scalp in order to reduce stress and promote hair growth.

15. Applying a few drops of tea tree oil and olive oil mixed together can soothe the skin after a shave.

16. Any rough areas of skin can be softened by massaging tea tree oil onto the area once a day.

17. Soaking your nails in a few cups of warm water with two to three drops of tea tree oil can help eliminate nail fungus and soften cuticles.

As you can see, tea tree oil has many uses for health and beauty. Give a few of these a try and see how it can improve your life. Keep a bottle on hand for when you need it.

Uses for Coconut Oil

Coconut oil has always been associated with nice-sounding products. It has a number of health benefits as well as beauty uses. Consider the following ways that depression-era women learned to use coconut oil for health and beauty.

1. Coconut oil is an easy make-up remover to clean off mascara. Place some on a cotton ball and brush gently around the eyes.

2. Coconut oil is used by moms to keep bottoms from getting red and irritated. Use a little bit at each diaper change.

3. Coconut oil helps keep the skin supple, and rubbing a few drops onto your belly and sides can prevent stretch marks.

4. Coconut oil has a natural SPF 5, and placing a few dabs on your skin can be used as an emergency sunscreen if you don't have any.

5. A few drops of coconut oil on your baby's scalp and rubbed in can help get rid of the cradle cap.

6. A few drops of coconut oil during a massage will make it more enjoyable.

7. Combing a few drops of coconut oil into your hair will keep it frizz-free.

8. Adding a few drops of coconut oil in your morning shake can improve your metabolism for the day.

9. Coconut oil added to a body scrub will have it smell great and add moisturizing properties.

10. Coconut oil can make your lips soft and moisturized. Apply some to chapped lips and see immediate results.

11. Coconut oil can be used in first aid for burns and minor cuts by protecting the wound and helping it heal faster.

12. Coconut oil rubbed daily on severe skin irritations such as psoriasis can alleviate symptoms.

13. A few drops of coconut oil on the tongue has been thought to improve mental function.

14. Swabbing coconut oil inside your nose can help reduce allergy symptoms.

15. Coconut oil can soothe an upset stomach and kill any internal parasites that result in digestion issues. Simply add a few drops to something you drink each day.

16. Applying coconut oil to sunburns can ease the pain and prevent peeling. Apply once a day until the burn is gone.

17. Comb coconut oil into hair to prevent lice.

18. Added to any lotion, coconut oil can improve moisturizing abilities.

19. Taking a teaspoon of coconut oil before each meal will help with digestion, prevent infections, and reduce the symptoms of many common ailments.

With so many benefits, it is easy to see why many used coconut oil on a daily basis. You can find it at most stores for an affordable price.

Uses for Witch Hazel

Witch hazel is a product that has a great many benefits. It has long been a frugal, all-natural folk remedy that became popular during the Great Depression. Consider the following uses for witch hazel and then make up a tincture and tea to use around your house.

1. Makeup Remover

2. Hemorrhoid Relief

3. Cleaning Wounds

4. Reducing Swelling and Inflammation

5. Treating Acne and Cleaning Oily Skin

6. Reduce Varicose Veins

7. Eliminate Puffiness Under-Eyes

8. Stop Itchiness

9. Dry Poison Ivy

10. Refine Pores

11. Astringent and Skin Refresher

12. Shampoo to Prevent Frizz

13. Balance Skin Moisture

14. Treat Dandruff

15. Reduce Redness and Pimples

16. Treat Chicken Pox Blisters

17. Soothe Sunburn

18. Prevent Razor Burn

19. Remove Bug Bite Irritation

20. Reduce Psoriasis and Eczema

21. Disinfectant and Sanitizer

Depression-era Lifehacks for Having Fun

There are plenty of ways to become frugal in your life and save money. However, this doesn't mean you can't have fun while saving money. Even during the Great Depression, families found ways to have fun and enjoy life. Let's consider how you can do things for free and how you can still enjoy the holiday while on a budget.

Free Things to Do

One thing families were great at doing during the Great Depression was finding ways to have fun while spending little to no money. There are plenty of options. First, consider things you can do within your own home to have fun.

1. Play a board game

2. Read a book

3. Listen to a podcast or audiobook

4. Do a puzzle

5. Take a free online learning course

6. Watch YouTube videos

7. Cook your meals or bake

8. Organize or clean a room

9. Watch a movie

10. Take up a craft

11. Start a workout routine

12. Look online for free items

13. Have a spa day

14. Take a nap

15. Write a book or blog

16. Start a journal

17. Put together a scrapbook

If none of these sounds appealing or if you simply are tired of staying around the house, then consider some free things you can do that gets you outside.

1. Go for a picnic

2. Take a jog

3. Go to the beach

4. Go fishing

5. Go camping

6. Take a bike ride

7. Fly a kite

8. Tour your city

9. Take a hike

10. Go swimming

11. Visit an open house

12. Take a free class at the community college

13. Go to a free concert

14. Go to the library

15. Make your own scavenger hunt

16. Take a drive in your car

17. Play a sport

Holidays on a Budget

Another area that is often important for families is being able to celebrate the holidays. Just because you are being frugal and living on a budget doesn't mean you can't still have a memorable holiday experience. Consider how you can enjoy the three main holidays of Thanksgiving, Christmas, and

New Year's on a budget.

Thanksgiving

Depending on the size of your family, Thanksgiving dinner may or may not be an easy thing to host frugally. However, no matter what size of dinner you are planning, there are ways to host a memorable and frugal dinner. Let's look at how you can do this.

Planning ahead and having a budget is the best way to have a frugal Thanksgiving dinner. This also gives you time to look for the best deals and sales on things you need.

Purchase vegetables at a farmer's market. Often the prices of vegetables are going to be less at a farmer's market. Thanksgiving dinners often have a lot of vegetable-based side dishes. When you save money on vegetables, you'll find it takes a lot out of your budget. If you don't have a farmer's market in your area, then look for sales at the grocery stores. If you can't find a fresh vegetable for cheap, then you can price frozen vegetables.

While a store-bought dessert may seem convenient, especially when you already have a lot of cooking to do, it can also be costly. If you have the time, make your own desserts ahead of time to save money. Not only will you save money, but homemade desserts also taste better.

Have family and friends bring side dishes as a potluck. This will save you money as well as preparation and cooking time. It also allows people to bring a special dish, and everyone gets to share something unique.

Avoid buying too much turkey by buying just enough to satisfy everyone's needs with just a small amount of leftovers. Turkeys are often the most expensive item of Thanksgiving, and buying the right amount can save you money. If you do buy too much, then make the most out of your leftovers and don't waste food.

Around Thanksgiving time, you'll often find local coupons and sales. Keep an eye out for these deals and buy whatever you can in advance such as sparkling cider, boxed stuffing, and crescent rolls.

Consider what you have at home first. You'll often find a lot of what you need at home. If there are decor items missing, make a list, and stick to it. Head to the Dollar Store first, where you're likely to find great savings on all the decor you need.

Christmas

Christmas is both a high cost but also a stressful holiday. You're expected to get gifts, prepare dinner, and entertain the family. In addition, it is just after you've spent money on Thanksgiving and are trying to save money for New Year's. Let's consider how you can save on Christmas just like people did during the Great Depression.

The best way to start any holiday planning is with a budget. Once you have a budget, outline what you need to buy and use what you have at home. Then make sure you stick within the budget. Once you go over budget, it will be difficult to get back on target.

After you have a budget in mind, then you can start putting together a menu of what you'll serve at Christmas dinner. This way, you can have a shopping list in advance. Buy anything you can in advance when it is on sale and save it. Also, be sure to check your pantry first and see if you already have some of the items you need.

Rather than trying new or elaborate dishes for the holiday,

stick with the basic dishes you know your family likes. This saves both money and time while reducing the risk of leftover food waste.

Family should be what matters during the holidays, and you shouldn't feel the need to impress anyone. So don't spend a lot of time and money on fancy things like invites and decor. Rather keep things simple and basic.

Just because you are hosting a family dinner doesn't mean you need to pay for it all on your own. If you have a family member that makes a great dish, ask them to provide it. You can even do a potluck dinner so everyone can help out with the dinner.

Christmas decor is often one area where people spend a lot of money, especially if they like to decorate. Consider saving money by making your own decor or set a strict budget for your decorating. Plus, save as many decorations as you can for the next year.

Another area where a lot of money is spent is on gifts. Focus on buying just one or two gifts per person. This will both save you money, but also remind you that the true meaning of Christmas is spending time with family and not gifting. If you have a larger family, then you may want to consider drawing names and having each person focus on just one person for gifting.

Depending on your party style, you may or may not need help in planning a frugal New Year's Party. For some, it is just a normal night, but for others, it is time for a big party. If you want to party on New Year's Eve, then consider the following tips to help you have a frugal one.

While having no alcohol would certainly save on your budget, this may not be a fun idea for some. Another option is to choose one type of drink and then find something that isn't too expensive or look for wholesale clubs that may have sales on cases.

For most parties, you won't need to provide more than finger foods and small cocktail treats. You can also plan your party for after dinner. This means most people will be full and not that interested in food. If you do want to have more food options, consider making it a potluck and having everyone bring something.

Keeping the number of people invited small can reduce costs and have a more relaxed atmosphere. You can also invite people digitally to save money on invites.

If possible, use leftover decor and staples from the previous holidays. Keep fireworks from July 4th for New Year's Eve and reuse things like Christmas lights. Coming out of Christmas, you'll also find a lot of sale deals to help you stock up on what you need.

Depression-era Hacks for Finding Things for Cheap or Free

A SEASONS SUPPLY FOR INDIAN CRAFT SHOP

Perhaps one of the best ways to live frugally and learn from people during the Great Depression is to save money on your spending. Often people in the Great Depression went without, and when they needed to get supplies, they found ways to do so cheaply. Let's look at how you can apply this to your lives today.

How to Save Money When Shopping

Part of being frugal is knowing how to save money while shopping. The best way to save money is by knowing what you should never pay full price for. There are certain things you can get for free or cheap as long as you take the time to look for them. Never pay full price for the following:

1. Digital song downloads. Often sites will allow you to download up and coming artists for free. You can also often find discounts on gift cards for purchasing digital music.

2. Laundry supplies are easy to make on your own. Save money per load by making your own laundry soap and avoid the harsh chemicals.

3. Electronic books. Often classic books will have expired copyrights and become easily available in electronic format. You can often find these at online bookstores. Plus, online sites like Amazon and Kindle may occasionally offer free downloads.

4. Clothing, especially for kids. Kids outgrow clothes fast, so you shouldn't pay full price for them. Rather

go to thrift stores to get what you need and pass them along once your kids outgrow them. This will save you a lot of money, but it will also give you a wide selection to choose from.

5. Magazines are fast becoming obsolete. If you still like to read the paper version, then head to the library. It also gives you a chance to get out of the house and have something free to do for a few hours.

6. Baby food can be quite costly, but you can save a lot of money by making your own. Nearly any food can be pureed in a food processor and turned into baby food.

7. Toothpaste and toothbrushes can often be found for free at your dentist's office. You can also make your own toothpaste with baking soda to save money.

8. Eating at restaurants can be costly, but it doesn't mean you have to always eat at home. Look for deals and coupons to save money when you eat out at a restaurant.

9. Scratched and dented items. When you go shopping, check out the clearance bin. Oftentimes the items are

fine; just have a minor blemish that means the store can't sell them for full price. If you find something damaged that isn't on sale, ask the store for a discount, and you'll probably get it.

Shopping Monthly Sales

Another great way to save money when shopping is to make sure you buy things when they are on sale. Retail stores follow a pattern in this regard. Each month there are specific items that go on sale. Stock up or wait to purchase these items when they are on sale.

- January

    - Linens, towels, sheets, curtains, and tablecloths.

    - Furniture.

    - Electronics.

- February

    - Jewelry

- Gift sets

- Large appliances

- March

  - Coats, hats, and gloves.

  - Travel discounts.

- April

  - Vacuums

  - Cars

- May

  - Mattresses

  - Electronics

  - Grills and outdoor gear.

- June

  - Menswear

- Tools

- Housewares

- July

  - Swimsuits, shorts, tanks, and tees.

  - Grills and grilling accessories.

  - School supplies.

- August

  - School and office supplies.

  - Lawnmowers, outdoor play items, and camping gear.

- September

  - Computers, laptops, and dorm room supplies.

  - Large appliances.

  - Outdoor gardening equipment and plants.

- October

- Air conditioning units

- Furniture

- Home decor

- November

  - Online shopping

- December

  - Gift sets

  - Body care items

  - Clothing

  - Food

Buying in Bulk

One of the biggest tips for when living frugally is to buy in bulk. However, for a lot of people, this may seem impossible because they feel they don't have the space or money to buy in bulk. It is important that you keep several things in mind when you buy in bulk, and these things might help you to see things differently. First, I'm going to discuss with you how to do bulk shopping, then I'll discuss what things are the best to buy at warehouse stores in bulk.

The Do's of Buying in Bulk

Before you choose to buy in bulk, you want to compare unit prices. Sometimes things that seem like a great deal may not really be a deal when you compare the cost per item. It is also important that you know the prices of items you typically buy in a store when they are on sale. If you can stock up on an item when it's on sale, and it will keep then wait for the sale to stock up. If needed, you can have a price book to help you keep track of prices.

You should also create a storage area for your bulk items. You'll find a range of organization options for keeping items in your home or garage. Use a variety of bins, shelves, and closets to help you organize everything.

Lastly, it is important that you only buy in bulk when you can save ten percent or more. You should also stick with buying items that you use a lot.

The Don'ts of Buying in Bulk

Never buy a product in bulk if you won't be able to use it up before it goes bad. There is no such thing as a good deal if it goes to waste.

Buying in bulk doesn't mean you need to buy everything at once. You can start buying in bulk with only a few items a month.

Lastly, don't feel you need to buy everything in bulk. There are some things that aren't a great deal, and you'll end up saving more buying them at a store with a coupon.

What to Buy at Warehouse Stores

When you decide to start buying bulk, it will typically be at warehouse stores. When shopping for items in bulk at warehouse stores, you should shop for the following items:

☐ Spices

☐ White Rice

☐ Nuts

- [ ] Condiments

- [ ] Meats

    - Ground Beef - Good for three months

    - Whole Chicken - Good for one year

    - Steaks - Good for six months

    - Roasts - Good for four months

    - Pork Chops - Good for six months

    - Whole Fish - Good for around six months

- [ ] Cooked Meat - Lasts for about three months in the freezer

- [ ] Vegetables and Fruits

- [ ] Paper Products

- [ ] Personal Hygiene Items

- [ ] Baby Supplies

- [ ] Cereal and Snacks

If you don't plan on buying in bulk or won't be able to eat things before they go to waste, then you should look for other ways to save money on groceries. Consider the following tips to help you save money on groceries.

More Ideas for Saving Money on Groceries

There are many tips and tricks you can use to shop frugally and save money when purchasing groceries. Perhaps one of the best tips is to purchase cheaper alternatives. When shopping on a budget, be sure to consider these alternatives.

Meats

Buy:

- Bulk Hamburger

- Whole Chickens

- Roasts

Don't Buy:

- Boneless Chicken Breasts

- Individual Pounds of Ground Beef

- Individual Steaks

Canned Goods

Buy:

- Tomato Sauce

- Tuna

Don't Buy:

- Canned Fruits

- Canned Vegetables

- Canned Pasta Sauce

In addition to these alternatives, consider the following tips to help you save money when grocery shopping:

Always have a game plan when shopping. Make a list of what

you need at the store and stick to the list when shopping. This will prevent you from overbuying. Having a meal prep menu in advance and checking your home before you go will ensure you only buy what you need and reduce money spent on buying too much food or going out to restaurants.

Also, keep your eyes on the sales. Grocery stores often have weekly sales flyers either online or in the paper. Use these ads to create your shopping lists and plan your meals. If you eat a particular item often and don't see it on sale too often, then stock up when you do find it on sale.

Using coupons is another great way to save. When you create a shopping list, combine it with coupons to increase the sales savings. Also, keep in mind the coupon policies of your local supermarket. Shop on days that double coupons are allowed and keep an eye out on coupons offered within the store itself.

If needed, purchase frozen fruits and vegetables if they are cheaper than fresh. It will also reduce waste since you can portion them out and store the rest in the freezer. Fresh produce doesn't last as long unless you can or preserve them in some other way. At the same time, you should always purchase in-season produce. This way, you can purchase at farmer's markets where you support the local economy and get a great deal on produce.

If possible, consider purchasing generic or store brand products. Often you pay for the big-named brands and can save money buying generic; often, there isn't much of a difference in the ingredients. Compare the two labels before making a decision; the nutritional value and ingredients should be nearly identical.

It is also important to shop at the right time. If possible, shop earlier in the day. At this time, the stores are less crowded, so shopping is quicker and reduces your chances of purchasing more than you intended. You should also avoid shopping when you are hungry or tired since you are more prone to buying foods that are high in carbs or sugars. If you shop while hungry, you're also more prone to buying too much. It is also a good idea to shop alone if you can, since bringing others can almost double your sending.

When you go shopping, you should use a smaller cart if possible. When you have a larger cart, you may feel the need to fill it; otherwise, you feel like you aren't getting enough. Shopping with a smaller cart leaves less room for impulse buys.

Lastly, consider if you can shop at non-traditional stores for groceries. In some areas, shopping at places like the Dollar Store for certain items can be cheaper than shopping at a grocery store. Let's consider what you should purchase when shopping at a Dollar Store to help you save money.

Shopping at the Dollar Store

Dollar Stores are a great place to find a deal. You will likely find pretty much anything you need here, including food. It is a good idea to check here for certain items before you purchase them somewhere else. Let's consider what you should purchase at a Dollar Store and what you should avoid.

What to Buy at Dollar Stores

- Cleaning Supplies

- Frozen Foods

- Seasonal Items

- Packing

- Party Supplies

- Beauty Supplies

What Not to Buy at Dollar Stores

- Baking Soda

- Flour

- Sugar

- Canned Goods

- Vitamins

- Beverages

- School Supplies

- Knives

All these tips and tricks are good at saving your money when you go grocery shopping, but during the Great Depression, there were individuals who couldn't afford any food.

What do you do if you find yourself in this situation? There are ways to find food for free.

Food Pantries

Whether you fall on hard times and run out of food or a food shortage leads to a lack of availability in your area; there may be times when you have no way to get food. Thankfully, there are plenty of places where you can look to find free food.

Food Banks

Nearly all communities have a food bank of some kind. You can utilize them to get food sometimes up to twice a month. They can be a great source of food when you are struggling and need a little help.

211

In most places in the United States, 211 provides assistance from any phone. You simply need to tell them what you are looking for, and they'll find you the right resources.

They can help put you in contact with charities in your area that can help supply you with groceries.

Local Churches

Sometimes the churches in your area have a way to organize food or gift card donations to help families in need. While they may not have a lot to provide, they may also be able to point you in the direction of organizations that can help.

Forage

Nearly anywhere you live, you can forage for food such as edible weeds, fruit, and mushrooms. Even in city areas, you can still find some options. It is best to have a guidebook on hand or keep a journal of your own with where you can find edible plants because you don't want to eat the wrong plants.

WIC and SNAP

Most people have heard of these programs, and they can be a great benefit for those in need. In addition to signing up for these services, be sure to ask about programs where you can use them.

Sometimes there are certain stores or farmer's markets where you are able to get more for your benefits than a regular grocery store.

While it is great to use these services, it will feel better when you can get a job and start providing for yourself and your family again. During the Great Depression, jobs were in short supply, and many people had to find unique ways to make money. Let's see how that applies to us today.

Depression-era Tips for Making Money without a Job

Everyone knows the importance of a savings account and

having money set aside for a rainy day. However, if you have to live paycheck to paycheck, then it can be a little difficult to add money to your savings or set money aside. There are plenty of ways you can start generating some extra income and help set aside money to get back on your feet. Consider five ways you can add extra money to your savings.

Extra Money Savings

The most obvious thing you can do is to save half of any extra money you get. This could be bonuses at work, birthday gifts, or any other payments you weren't expecting. Set half of these amounts aside in your savings. Often this is extra money you weren't expecting as a part of your budget, so saving it wouldn't be that hard. It may not seem like a lot, but even an extra $5 each time will add up to a large amount in your savings at the end of the year.

Save Your Change

Start paying in cash and when you come home at the end of the day, put your coin change in a jar. At the end of the year, you'll be surprised how much money you have set aside in a jar. Depending on your bank, you may also get a bonus if you put your change into your savings account.

Unused Gift Cards

You probably have several gift cards lying around your house that just have a few dollars on them. If you have these, you may be able to cash them in at retailers or through gift card sales kiosks in most stores.

Phone Apps

There are plenty of apps available on your phone that allows you to save money on groceries and household items. This will give you extra money to save. Some of these apps will also give you rebates and bonuses for using their services.

Talk to Your Bank

If you have a direct deposit for your paycheck, most banks will allow you to auto-save a certain amount from each check when it is deposited. Some banks will also round up debit purchases and put the extra into your savings. This can add up easily, depending on how many purchases you make and the amount you have set aside from your paychecks. Best of all, since you don't see the amount yourself, you won't be tempted to spend it, and it will be automatically saved for you.

If none of these options work for you, then you still have options open to you for getting extra money. Perhaps one of the best options is to sell items around your home for cash.

Selling Items for Cash

If you need to get extra money or just want to build up your savings, then look no further than your own home. A lot of people aren't aware of just how many items in their home are worth a lot of money. Consider the most common household items that you can sell for cash.

- ☐ Soda cans or other aluminum products can be taken to your local recycling center. The products are weighed, and you are given cash right away.

- ☐ If you drink wine, then save your wine corks. You can sell them online for those who use them in craft projects. You may also be able to sell the empty wine bottles as well if they are decorative or something a collector may be interested in having.

- If you have real silver, then you can cash in on it, no matter what condition. Go to a local jeweler who is buying silver, and after weighing it, they'll give you cash for your silver.

- Another option is jewelry that is made from gold. Again you can cash in on it no matter what the condition. As with your silver, take it to a jeweler who can weigh it and make you an offer. This is a great way to get rid of any jewelry you don't wear anymore.

- If you had children and they've outgrown their clothes, you can sell these for cash. If you have gently used clothing items and accessories, then most local resale stores will give you cash for them.

- The same also applies to your own clothing. Look for local consignment shops in your area and get rid of clothing you don't wear anymore as long as it is in good shape. You should also go through your accessories since shoes, belts, and purses can be sold for cash as well.

- Perhaps you have collectibles or knick-knacks that you don't use or need. Collectors love to purchase these items, and you can often take them to local antique shops to see if there is any interest.

☐ Just because a video game system is upgraded doesn't mean there is no value in old video games. Gather up video games you don't play anymore and take them to a buyback store or sell them online. People will often purchase video games for cash and may be interested in what you have to offer.

☐ Books are still popular with the right people. Sell any books you no longer plan to read on Amazon or other online auction sites. Collectors and avid readers are likely to purchase your books.

☐ Take the time to look through your closets and other storage areas. You'll likely find a number of odds and ends that you didn't know you still had. You can gather these items together and have a yard sale.

☐ Perhaps you'll find you have old and broken cell phones hiding in these areas. Most don't realize you can sell these for cash. There are plenty of people online that will pay cash for old cell phones of all kinds.

- The best item that sells second hand at a great price is tools. This includes both power tools and hand tools. You can sell these online or in your local paper or online sale sites.

- Another great place to look is your kitchen. You'll probably notice that there are a couple appliances you don't use anymore. You'll be able to sell most of these online at a great price while reducing clutter in your kitchen.

- Unused gift cards are a great source of cash. You can often sell them for about 75% of their value online. Or you can use the cards yourself.

Once you have collected items from your home to sell, you'll often need to head online to sell them. Let's consider how you can sell stuff online to get the most money for your items.

How to Sell Online

After decluttering your home, you'll likely have a number of excess items. While donating is a quick and easy way to get rid of these items, you can also sell some items to get some extra money. While this isn't the most profitable option, it is an easy option to get a little side money. Consider the following tips to help you have success when selling online.

Sell Quality Items

Think of the items you are trying to sell; do you feel they hold value, or do you view them as junk? If you view them as junk, then most other people will too, and you aren't likely to get money for them. Never try to sell items that are broken, ripped, torn, or unusable; it is better to just recycle or throw away these items. The only exception is if it is an old item that has collectible value.

Clean Things Up

Before you list an item for sale, you should clean it up as best as you can. Remove any stains if possible and clean off visible dust and dirt. Clean items will always sell quicker and at higher prices than dirty items. Again the only exception is antique or vintage items that either have a natural patina or require special cleaning. Some of these items are worth more with their natural patina if they aren't cleaned.

Detailed Photos

When selling things online, the photo is the main selling point. This means you need detailed photos if you want your item to sell quickly for top dollar. Try to photograph items from every angle and then document any cosmetic issues with photos that are lit enough to see well. The better the listing photos, the more you are likely to get. Also, avoid using stock photos of items.

Fair Prices

When it comes to selling items online, one of the main reasons people aren't successful is because they are pricing too close to retail. If people can purchase the same item, new, for just a few dollars more, then they aren't going to want your used one. Rather prices should be set about 50 to 75 percent below retail depending on how often they are used and how well they hold up as a used item.

Meet Locally If Needed

If you are selling locally, then make sure you are willing to meet the buyer. You can always get more sales when you are willing to meet individuals. Just make sure you pick somewhere that is halfway, in public, and safe.

Choose Where to Sell

There are a number of places online where you can sell items: eBay, OfferUp, LetGo, and Facebook Marketplace, to name a few. You can list your items in more than one place at a time, but if you do this, make sure you monitor your listing closely and remove an item from all locations the moment it sells.

Detailed Descriptions

Lastly, a key to selling items is to have a well-written item description. Rather than simply saying what the item is, you should be detailed about any issues it has, what you paid for it, and more relevant details. The more information you provide, the more people you will attract, and the faster you can sell an item. It is also important that you use proper grammar, so people aren't confused by what you're trying to say.

Generating Side Income

In addition to selling things online, another option for

making money that was learned during the Great Depression is to have a side income. Our grandparents had to get creative when it came to finding ways to support a family. If you find yourself struggling to make ends meet today, then you'll likely want to look for side jobs that will bring in money based on your talents and availability. Many of the side jobs during the Great Depression can still be done today.

Babysitting

This classic job isn't just for teenagers. In most states, you don't need a license in order to babysit unless you are watching more than just a few kids. Check with your state to see how many unrelated kids under the age of 2 can be watched at a time. You'll also want to see if there are any specific laws in your state. This is a great way to bring in extra cash, especially if you work from home or aren't currently employed outside of the home.

Mending Clothes

This is a nearly forgotten talent since most of the world is used to throwing away old or worn items. If you can mend clothing, you could be making some decent side income. Most people don't want to throw away expensive items during hard times and will gladly pay to have them mended if it saves money on the cost of purchasing a replacement.

Sell Items

As we already covered, selling items you don't need or want anymore can bring in money. You can sell online or hold a garage sale. You can also find free items in your area or at thrift stores; with a little cleaning and fixing, you can then sell the item for some side money.

Write a Blog

If you want to work from home and make a side income, then you can start writing a blog. You can even make a comfortable full-time income doing this. However, you will have to put in some work to make this happen. With blogging, the great option is that you can continue to make passive income once you get it started.

Start a Business Online

It is becoming easier to sell retail items and make a profit on sites like social media. With just a few clicks, you can start an online business with dropshipping as an option, so you don't even need to have inventory on hand.

Tutoring

Do you have a degree in English, do you enjoy doing math, or can you play an instrument? In most states, no special training or license is needed in order to tutor kids in subjects. This can be a great side income for college students while they go to school or can be another great option for those who aren't employed outside of the home.

Housecleaning

People are busy, and many people try to budget for a housekeeper to help reduce the chores they need to do. You can often make a couple hundred dollars a month with just a few hours of cleaning. You can sometimes even find regular work by cleaning out apartment complexes after people move out or cleaning business offices. However, to do this job, you will need to be bonded, licensed, and insured. But this process doesn't cost a lot and is fairly quick.

Sell Homemade Items

Do you like crafting? Do you spend your free time making

homemade items? If this is the case, have you considered selling these items? You can get paid good money to sit at home and do your favorite crafts and hobbies; what could be better? You can even personalize items for people to increase their chances of purchasing. The options for this side income are endless such as crafts, food, cakes, ice cream, soaps, etc.

Complete Errands

Sometimes people don't have time to run errands. Other people are homebound and unable to get out of the house to run errands. When you run errands for others, you can make a little money on the side. You can also offer to deliver grocery food.

Freelancing

This is a great option for making some money on the side. You won't find it to be as passive as a blog, but it can be a way to make quick cash. It can be a range of services such as writing, photography, graphic design, etc. The best part is you can do most of these jobs from home.

Stock Investments

Another great way to make some side money is to invest in stocks. However, make sure you choose the right time to cash out should the economy start having problems.

Start a Business

While this may not seem like a viable option in a depression, it can be a source of side income. However, this is a way to make side income that may turn into the main income if everything works out well. Just remember this option takes a lot of commitment.

Depression-era Budgeting Ideas

In addition to making extra money or learning to get creative with ways to support your family, it is also a good idea to maintain a budget. Having a budget will allow you to set money aside in case you need it while also ensuring all of your needs get met.

How to Develop a Successful Budget

Budgeting can be a great way to manage money, but for some, it is a difficult and dreadful thing. It can be difficult to start since people may feel it takes too much time, or they aren't sure how to do it effectively. Consider the following tips to help you get started on your way to creating a successful budget.

Keep It Simple

There are a number of electronic apps and websites that can provide you with the tools needed to understand your budget and see what's going in and out of your bank account. If you have a simple budget, you'll find the process is a lot easier. This is especially true if it is available on your computer.

Use Broad Categories

When setting up a budget, remember you don't have to micromanage everything. Rather you can use broad categories for your most frequent expenses. For example, food, mortgage/rent, utilities, automobile, entertainment, savings, etc. When you are less specific, you are able to simplify things and make it easier to stick with your budget.

Ensure You Can Stick with It

If you make your budget planning overly complicated, you're less likely to stick with your budget. So when starting your budget, make sure you are honest with yourself. If you don't feel you can stick with a portion of your budget, then think of a different solution.

Finish the Boring Stuff First

When creating a budget, you first need to know where your money is going. To do this, don't actively budget for about a month or two. Rather just watch where your money is going and make notes; be completely honest with yourself. At the end of the month, you can look through your notes. This can help you decide what to do next and help you to create an effective budget.

Make It Easy to Save

For a lot of people, the easiest option here is to set up automatic savings. If you have a direct deposit for your paycheck, you can have your bank put a portion of it into your savings account. This means you won't even have to think about this step since it is all done automatically.

Set Up an Allowance

In order to avoid needless spending, you should consider setting up an allowance for yourself. Even if you don't do anything else to budget, this should be a big one. When you have a weekly spending budget and only carry enough cash for this, then you'll stop spending on things you don't need, and you'll improve the likelihood of being able to stick with a budget and live within your means.

Budget by Envelopes

This option is for those who have a hard time with electronic billing and need extra motivation to stay within their means. Cash your paycheck and then put specific amounts of money in envelopes labeled with their purposes: one for each bill, food, savings, etc. This will make your spending more organized and will ensure you have enough money for all your needs.

Set Aside Some for Yourself

The biggest reason most people don't stick to a budget is that they don't like living with just the bare essentials. So make sure you set aside a specific amount each paycheck that you can put towards entertainment, shopping, or dining out; then make a splurge once a month or once a paycheck. You'll be able to control your spending while still avoiding the feeling of being deprived or unhappy.

Creating a budget is certainly the best way to keep yourself above water financially. As you can see from above, it is a simple enough task; but it can take some practice and getting used to in order to find what works best for you. We should also consider some of the main reasons why budgeting tends to fail so you can prepare and avoid these roadblocks.

Reasons Budgets Fail

Estimating

Perhaps the biggest way a budget can fail is if you don't take an honest look at your spending and simply just estimate. You may think that you only spend $300 a month on food, but if you aren't counting eating out and short trips to pick up items that were forgotten, then you may be overspending. For the first month or two of budgeting, you should keep a close record of all food purchases you make and see how much you spend versus what you budgeted for the food category.

Forgetting Things

Many people are good at remembering to budget in monthly expenses since they happen regularly. However, a lot of times, people forget to include annual or semi-annual expenses in their budgeting, such as property taxes or life insurance. You'll also want to make sure you leave room for less common expenses such as vehicle maintenance, doctor co-pays, and other such expenses. The best way to avoid forgetting things is to take a look at your expenses from last year and see how much you may need to set aside in a specific month or by a certain point.

Meeting Your Needs

You also need to make sure you have a budget that is realistically meeting your needs. You may find you are allocating too much or too little for something. It is important to track your spending habits to see where there may be errors.

A Complicated Budget

It is possible to have a budget that is too complicated. Perhaps it is too hard to stick with, or it has too many things. Any of these things can make it harder to stick to a budget. Rather try to keep it simple, so you have an easier time working within your budget.

Too Many People

The best rule of thumb when it comes to budgeting is to have one person responsible for handling the budget. This means the individual can oversee everything, and you won't go outside of the budget. If you have too many people working on it, things can easily get overlooked or missed.

Spending More than You Make

Perhaps the most guaranteed way to destroy a budget is to live outside your means. There are plenty of ways to cut expenses, as we've discussed to help you stay within your finances. Perhaps something as simple as taking lunch to work. Doing whatever you can to stay within your financial means will help you stick to a budget easier.

Not Saving Anything

A part of any budget is to save some of your paycheck and not spend it all each month. The budget can only work so well if you live paycheck to paycheck. It is important to set money aside, so you have something left for a "rainy day" or an emergency in case you do find yourself needing to go over budget at some point. Having funds in reserve will help you recover without completely ruining your budget.

Talk to Others

It is important that all members of the house know that you are setting up a budget and what it entails. This way, everyone can figure out together where the money needs to go. Consider having an expense log where others can see it so that everyone can be in agreement on what to purchase and when.

Having No Rewards

Budgeting is hard, but it is even more difficult if you don't give you something for yourself and make sure you have a chance to have fun. While you should save and focus on expenses, make sure you also give yourself some money to set aside for entertainment. If you don't do this, then budgeting will quickly feel like you're doing it for nothing, and you'll end up cutting into other parts of your budget to have a little fun.

The Psychology of Poverty

Being poor, living paycheck to paycheck, being unable to support yourself or your family; all of these things can have a big impact on people's emotional well being. During the Great Depression, as well as today, it is important to look at the psychological effects and learn how you can keep yourself healthy during these challenging times.

How People Coped During the Great Depression

As you can see from this book, people coped with the Great Depression in a variety of ways; but mostly by being creative and industrious. They found ways to do without and make do with what they had. Even though they didn't have much, they still found ways to enjoy life and have some fun.

Books were popular during the Great Depression because they allowed people to escape from their daily lives. They also used movies as a way to get away from reality. More importantly, they focused on spending time together and the family through things like board games and listening to music. Many of these things we can still do today.

While the world has changed a lot since the Great Depression, not much has changed in how you can cope with trying times. Let's look at how you can cope today.

How People Can Cope Today

When economic troubles arise and people start living frugally, one thing that can develop is known as frugal fatigue. You can begin to get worn down when you sacrifice for too long, live under restrictive budgets, and try to avoid spending money. In some cases, this can be reflected by the harmless activity of spending more to make up for denying yourself. However, it can also lead to serious health issues like depression. So it is important that we take the time to look at how you can overcome these feelings.

Focus on What You Have

Take a good look at what you already have in your life. Oftentimes, the feeling of fatigue simply comes from wanting something else while you have something that fills that gap just fine. Before you start feeling like you're denying yourself, consider some of the following things you probably already have in your life:

- ☐ Good Food

- ☐ Home Comforts

- ☐ Family

- ☐ Friends

- ☐ Health

- ☐ A Home

- ☐ Books

- ☐ Parks

- ☐ Occasional Treats

When you take the time to consider what you already have, you may find out you have more than you thought. Take the time to focus your energy on being grateful for what you have rather than looking for something you don't have.

Small Splurges

Another great way to avoid fatigue is to have small splurges planned. Each month put some money aside for a "splurge fund." This means you can do something fun once a month or keep saving up the money for a bigger splurge. Rather than waiting until you're burned out and making a big splurge, you should focus on a few small splurges when they have the least impact on your budget. This can help you feel like you are enjoying life without ruining your financially frugal lifestyle. Consider a few small splurges you can make:

- ☐ Enjoy an ice cream

- ☐ Buy a new book

- ☐ Go to a movie

- ☐ Buy a piece of sports equipment

- ☐ Get a new video game

There is any number of small splurges you can make, and with so many coupons services today, you can probably even save money on your splurge to help you stay safely within your budget. When you take this time for yourself, then you'll be less likely to give up your frugal living habits.

Use Discounts

You can also find ways to enjoy life and avoid fatigue by finding discounted activities. You can find discount passes to amusement parks or join deal sites to give you daily access to great deals.

There are likely also great deals around town. Some cities have summer concerts in the park, and you can always use the library to check out books and movies. Plus, you can always get out for a hike, camping, or biking. There may also be free museum days and free days for kids to eat at local restaurants. All of these options can help you have a frugal budget while still having fun.

The Difference Between Frugal and Cheap

This topic has been debated, but it is actually pretty simple. You just need to ask yourself two questions.

First, is the less expensive choice worth the extra time and money? If you are getting an item for cheaper, but you need to drive across town and spend more money on gas and time, then it may not be a frugal choice. It is just being cheap.

Second, what is the quality of the less expensive item? If a less expensive item is so cheap that it doesn't have value and can actually have a negative impact on your happiness, then you should avoid it.

The Benefits of a Frugal Lifestyle

There are a lot of benefits you can enjoy from living a frugal life. Consider just a few to help you see that living a frugal lifestyle is actually worth the time and effort you put into it.

- ☐ A sense of satisfaction from achieving your goals.

- ☐ Getting the best value when spending your hard-earned money.

- ☐ Enjoying the things you already own.

- ☐ Learning new skills.

- ☐ Helping to preserve the natural environment.

- ☐ Learning creative problem-solving skills.

Remember it is a Choice

You may face pressure from people who want you to live a certain way or spend your money on specific things. While it may not always be easy to take the frugal route, if you are confident in your choice to live frugally, then it can be easier.

Keep in mind that living frugally doesn't mean you need to pressure others to do the same. At the same time, you want your family and friends to respect your own financial choices. In some ways, frugal living can be viewed as deprivation, leading to a feeling of resentment. You can also choose to view frugal living as a happy choice. The decision is entirely up to you.

It Isn't All or Nothing

Frugal living is about finding a balance between three things:

1. High quality - high price versus low quality - low price

2. Needs versus wants

3. Consumerism versus minimalism

However, you don't have to live in the balance between each of these. It is okay to sometimes be on the cheap side of things while other times, it is okay to splurge on something extra expensive. The goal is to see yourself continually moving in a frugal living direction.

Spending Errors to Avoid

No one is expected to always make the frugal choice when it comes to spending. Sometimes you just need to give in to your wants, or you are in a hurry and need to make a quick decision that may not be the best. It is okay that this happens as long as you continue to meet your savings goals and don't go into debt. Keep in mind you aren't looking for perfection; you're just looking for a frugal trend. There are five things you need to do to avoid making spending errors.

If you're reading this book, you probably already have a desire or need to live a frugal life. However, it isn't easy or quick to switch to this focus. When you are first starting to live frugally, you'll find nearly every deal there is; but there are still a few traps that you can fall into that can ruin your chances of successfully living frugally.

Buying the Wrong Items in Bulk

This is the most common trap. You see something in bulk and look at the cost. You quickly calculate the per-item cost, and you think it is a great savings, so you buy it. Then a few months later, you find you still have the majority left; but no desire to use it or it has expired. Anyone who has ever shopped at Costco knows this. So make sure you follow the tips we already mentioned when you shop in bulk.

Losing Track of Free Trials

Nearly everyone has signed up for a free trial at one time or another. You have likely also forgotten to cancel at the end of the trial period. If you're fortunate, you only end up paying for an extra month of something that you didn't use past the first week. Avoid this by simply setting a reminder for yourself to cancel any free trial subscriptions you signed up for.

Forgetting After-Purchase Rebates

After-purchase rebates can be a great source of saving money, but they require a little work. However, for most people, once they get an item home, they never take the time to mail-in rebate forms. Perhaps sometimes the rebate is for a reward other than money, and it could even be a reward you don't want. The main thing is that you should focus on buying products that have in-store rebates, so you get all of your savings upfront.

Always Read the Fine Print

Whenever you find a deal or coupon, make sure you read the fine print. Otherwise, you may find out you aren't getting that good of a deal, or perhaps you'll end up paying full price since you don't want to hassle with the hoops you have to jump through for the deal.

Lower Quality for Cheaper Prices

As we've already discussed, make sure you don't confuse being frugal with being cheap. There is a big difference between these two. You need to find the balance between the time and effort you put into finding a deal and the actual price you are paying for something. You should also make sure you aren't sacrificing quality in order to save some money; this is especially true if it isn't something you need right away.

Now that we've talked about what frugal fatigue is and how to avoid it. Let's also look at some ways that you can get over depression without taking medications.

Ways to Boost Your Mood without Medication

Do Something New

Science has proven that when you try new things, it changes your level of dopamine. This is a chemical in the brain that impacts pleasure and enjoyment. So what new stuff should you try? It is really simple; just take a new route to work, go for a different lunch, watch a video about a hobby and try it out, wear something you haven't in a while or find new free events in your neighborhood. There are a lot of options.

Get Outside

Sunlight is known to boost mood and Vitamin D levels to help fight depression. If you live in a place without a lot of sun, consider buying a lightbox.

Be Grateful

Studies have shown that a daily ritual involving gratitude can have the same effect as chemical antidepressants. This can be accomplished by doing something as simple as writing down the things you are thankful for or mentally focusing on what you already have.

Remember, in order for this to be successful, you need to have it as a regular practice and not something that you randomly do once in a while. Set an alarm on your phone or use other reminders to do it each day.

Be Social

When you feel depressed, the first notion is to isolate

yourself from others. However, it is important to avoid this desire and rather try to be as social as possible.

When you spend time with others, it can be a big defense against depression. If you can't go out and be social, then you can join online support groups or call someone on the phone.

Eat Regularly

It is important you don't skip meals when feeling depressed. Stable blood sugar levels help you to maintain a stable mood. Low blood sugar often comes with feelings of depression, even if you don't have clinical depression.

Eat Right

It is also important that you eat food that can increase serotonin levels in your brain in order to decrease the symptoms of depression.

According to studies, this should be a high protein diet with foods that are rich in omega-3 fatty acids such as salmon, sardines, herring, mackerel, and anchovies. You should also focus on foods and oil with healthy fats such as coconut oil, flaxseed oil, eggs, and avocados.

Stay Hydrated

If you aren't well hydrated, then your body will become fatigued. Fatigue can often mimic the symptoms of depression. Therefore, it is important to make sure you are drinking enough water.

There are several things you can do to help you increase your water intake. Perhaps you need a bottle that keeps water cold for 24 hours, or maybe you need a bottle that measures how much you are drinking throughout the day. No matter what you need to do, just make sure you are staying well hydrated throughout the day.

Enjoy Green Tea

Depression and caffeine aren't a good mix since it leads to a high, followed by a crash. However, the caffeine in green tea works along with L-theanine to prevent the caffeine crash while still lifting your mood a bit. It will also boost dopamine levels to help you feel better.

Meditate

Meditate is simply a way to be present and mindful of your

moment-to-moment experience. You can do this, both sitting still or while walking. Simply train your body, heart, and mind to be with whatever comes around you and provide you with the unconscious tools you need to navigate your life. Many studies have proven that meditation can help get rid of the symptoms of depression.

Do Yoga

This is something you can do in the comfort of your own home. The synchronized movement with your breathing can have great benefits for your mental and physical health. There are many styles and types of yoga to choose from, and they all work for your health, so try them all until you find one that works best for you.

Get Exercise

You've probably heard a lot about how exercise helps depression, and this is because it has been proven to work. When your heart rate increases, it releases endorphins that help to improve your mood.

Plus, exercise provides other physical benefits as well. It can be hard to get motivated to exercise when you're depressed, so you could invite someone to go with you. This will double the benefits of exercise and being social.

Change Positions

Sitting or lying in one spot for too long can make depression worse. So take the time to stand up, go for a walk, or do something that changes your position. Getting the blood flowing allows you to feel more connected to your body. This can increase confidence and lower stress hormones.

Smile More

Depression doesn't make you feel like smiling. However, even putting on a fake smile can help change the chemistry in your brain and get the good chemicals flowing. So remember to smile during the day to help you feel better, even if it is a fake smile.

Get Creative

When you perform creative activities, they can use your brain in different ways. These activities can help reduce the symptoms of depression. Some studies have even shown that creative activities produce similar effects to meditation.

Being creative doesn't mean you need to be good at it; just try something like writing, drawing, painting, cooking, knitting, or crafting.

Conclusion

Living a frugal lifestyle and learning from our grandparents during the Great Depression is a great idea for those who are living paycheck to paycheck. However, it can also be a great thing for those who simply want to get ahead and be prepared should another depression come. Although many people aren't ready to make the change to a frugal lifestyle. Hopefully, reading this guide will help you determine to make changes and start preparing for what is to come.

If this book has helped you in any way, and I sincerely hope it has, would you please leave a review where you purchased the book online? I would really appreciate it.

Made in the USA
Las Vegas, NV
06 December 2024

13467088R10118